NOTORIOUS MISSOURI

NOTORIOUS MISSOURI

200 YEARS OF HISTORIC CRIMES

JAMES W. ERWIN & VICKI BERGER ERWIN

Published by The History Press
Charleston, SC
www.historypress.com

First published 2021

ISBN 9781540246875

Library of Congress Control Number: 2020951646

CONTENTS

Contents

INTRODUCTION AND ACKNOWLEDGEMENTS

On February 8, 2007, Jim took the dog for her regular evening walk. Sirens blared—first one, then another and another and another. He stopped to talk to a neighbor. She said she heard that there was some kind of trouble at the City Hall—a shooting. A shooting in the quiet St. Louis suburb of Kirkwood?

Jim hurried home. He and Vicki locked the door and turned on the television. That's when the horrible news began to dribble out. There had been a shooting at Kirkwood City Hall. Six people were killed, including city council members, a city official, police officers and the shooter. The mayor died a few months later from his injuries. They knew some of the victims. They know people who were there under fire and who survived, scarred by what they saw and endured. They talked about whether they should—whether they could—write about this "notorious crime." They decided it must be done, but it was the most difficult part of this book to research and write.

The Kirkwood City Hall shooting was not the inspiration or motivation for writing this book, but it did remind Jim and Vicki that each of the crimes they wrote about here was its own tragedy. They were tragedies not only for the victims, but for the families and friends of the victims and perpetrators. Their experience with a tragedy that occurred in their own town, just a few blocks from where they live, reminded them that the people they wrote about were not just names on the page. They found their stories interesting, sometimes quirky, sometimes even funny in a bizarre sort of way, but they are, at their roots, tragic.

One of the crimes, the Mortimer murder in Mexico, Missouri, took place in Vicki's hometown but long before her time. She knew nothing about this unsolved murder until after moving away. She chose to write about that crime and the unsolved McDaniel murder in St. Joseph because they were so similarly described in the press. Both were considered notorious and heinous likely because they were perpetrated against society women. The Mortimer crime is an excellent example of the mores of the thirties: a black man was seen in the area where the murder occurred, so black men were considered the primary suspects. In fact, there is nothing to say that anyone else was ever looked at. The Missouri State Highway Patrol was in charge of the investigation, but it has no information on the crime available today. It's perplexing. The suggestion that the suspect was a transient sounds good until one is reminded that there were two similar crimes that took place before the murder with no suspects. The suspects in the McDaniel murder were first thought to have been men the victim's husband had dealt with, and the likely motive was revenge—until the prosecutor himself became the suspect. He was not convicted, and that murder, too, remains unsolved. The third unsolved murder—that of William Owens—is fairly characteristic of crime on the frontier. Suspects were arrested and set free on bond, only to disappear and never be heard from again. All armchair detectives "investigate" these unsolved cases in the hopes that a solution will magically appear.

Crime is an interesting topic, and there are always certain questions lurking below the surface. Why did this happen? Why did the perpetrator act? And probably most overarching: Could this happen to me?

The authors had to conduct the research for their last book on steamboats during a summer of floods. They researched and wrote this book during a pandemic. Thankfully, many institutions and publications have material online, making possible something that couldn't have been done a few years ago. Most of the authors' sources came from newspaper stories that were printed as the tales unfolded. There were too many to list them all individually in the bibliography, but if readers are interested, they are posted on the authors' websites.

The authors wish to thank the following persons for their assistance in finding information, illustrations and photographs: Dave and Lucy Tobben for suggesting the William Owens case; Marc Housman and the Washington, Missouri Historical Society for providing Owens's portrait; Lori Pratt and Janis Robison from the Audrain County Historical Society for providing the Margaret Mortimer materials; Charles Brown and Nick Fry for providing photographs from the *St. Louis Globe-Democrat* Collection at the Mercantile Library at the University of Missouri–St. Louis; Arlene Witterbee Muehlemann and Michael Huntington for the Morse Mill photographs, even though we weren't able to use them; Reuben Hemmer for the D&G Tavern photograph; the Missouri Historical Society; the State Historical Society of Missouri; and the Missouri State Archives. Finally, the authors would like to thank Chad Rhoad, Ashley Hill and everyone at The History Press for their patience and support. Of course, any errors are ours alone.

1.

DUELS AND GUNFIGHTS

Gunfights have been a part of Missouri history since the state's territorial days. Arguments over politics or gambling or almost any dispute, no matter how petty, often resulted in one person—or two—deciding to end it with a gun. In Missouri's territorial days and during its early days of statehood, gunfights between the elites were dignified as "duels" or even "interviews." Gunfights between the lower classes were just gunfights. Duelists tried to find secluded spots to vindicate their honor, but after the Civil War, the gunfights we now see popularized in modern media moved to the town square—and the first of those took place in Missouri.

"A PERSONAL INTERVIEW": THE BENTON-LUCAS DUELS

Duels were ostensibly banned by territorial and state laws, but the political and legal elite of Missouri in the nineteenth century did not let such things as mere laws keep them from the so-called field of honor. Many of the settlers of the new Missouri Territory came from the Upper South—Virginia, Tennessee and Kentucky—where the *code duello* was still a vital force. The best-known duels of the time involved Missourians from those states.

Thomas Hart Benton was born in North Carolina. He later moved to Nashville, Tennessee, where he became a successful planter and lawyer and a protégé of Andrew Jackson. However, trouble brewed between them when Jackson agreed to serve as the second in a duel between Benton's brother,

Thomas Hart Benton, Missouri's first senator, served for thirty years. His greatest regret was goading Charles Lucas into a second and fatal duel. *Courtesy of the Library of Congress.*

Jesse, and William Carroll. Jesse was a notoriously bad shot, and his round only nicked Carroll in the thumb. Jesse crouched to receive Carroll's shot and was shot, as one of Benton's early biographers put it, in a prominent "part of the body which is not supposed to be shot in duels."

Because of his wound, Jesse became, so to speak, the butt of jokes in Nashville, fueled by Jackson's retelling of the event. The bad blood between them culminated in a melee at a Nashville hotel, at which either Thomas or Jesse Benton shot Jackson in the arm. On realizing that being involved in Jackson's wounding would finish any of his ambitions in Tennessee, Benton moved to St. Louis. He quickly became one of the city's leading lawyers and a political force through his ownership of the second newspaper established in the territory.

Charles Lucas was the hothead son of John Baptiste Charles Lucas, one of the most prominent Missourians during the territorial era. Charles nearly fought a duel with another prominent Missourian, John Scott, over newspaper articles he wrote in connection with the 1814 election of the territorial representative to Congress. In the end, cool heads mediated the affair without gunplay, but Lucas sneered, "Mr. Scott thought it better that his honor should bleed, than that he should." However, Thomas Hart Benton, Lucas's next opponent, was not swayed from taking up arms.

Benton and Lucas first clashed in a court case, highlighted by mutual accusations of lying in the customary lofty tones of the day: "I contradict you, sir." "I contradict *you*, sir." Demands flew back and forth, but nothing violent—other than language—came of it.

The next year found the men on opposite sides of the 1817 election for the territorial representative in Congress, a rematch between Rufus Easton (Lucas's preferred candidate) and John Scott (Benton's man). Lucas claimed that Benton should not be able to vote because he failed to pay the taxes due on his three slaves. When queried about the allegation, Benton replied, "Gentlemen, if you have any questions to ask, I am prepared to answer, but I do not propose to answer charges made by any puppy who may happen to run across my path."

Lucas could not, of course, in the customs of the day, allow such an insult to pass. He wrote Benton a note, demanding "that satisfaction which is due from one gentleman to another for such an indignity." They named their seconds, who settled on the terms of what they called "a personal interview" between Benton and Lucas.

On August 12, 1817, Benton and Lucas met on Bloody Island, in the Mississippi River near St. Louis. The island got its well-deserved name

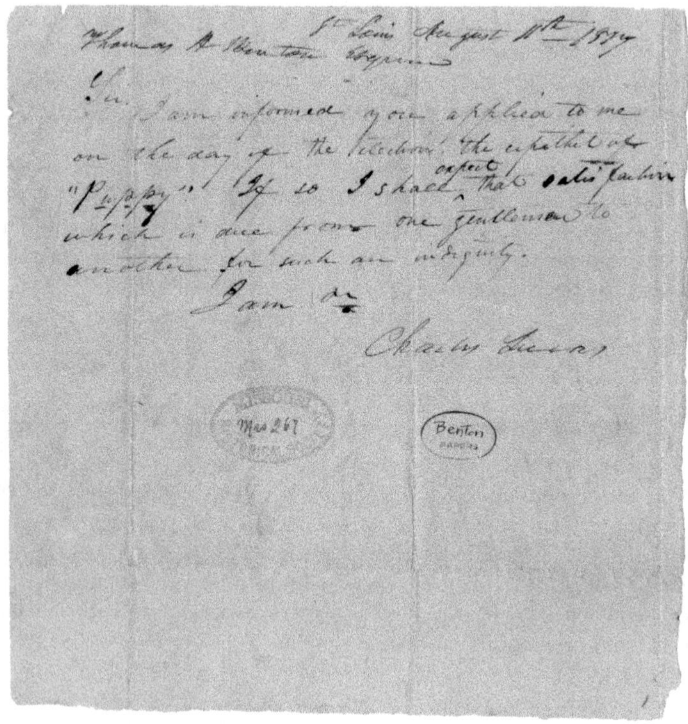

St Louis August 11th 1817

Thomas H. Benton Esquire

Sir,

I am informed you applied to me on the day of the election the epithet of "Puppy." If so I shall expect that satisfaction which is due from one gentleman to another for such an indignity.

I am Sir

Charles Lucas

Charles Lucas's letter challenging Thomas Hart Benton to a duel for calling him a "puppy." *Courtesy of the Missouri Historical Society.*

because it was a favorite place for resolving affairs of honor, as it was convenient to St. Louis and considered neutral ground. Both men fired from thirty paces. Benton was grazed just below the right knee. Lucas, however, was seriously wounded when the ball entered his neck. There was talk of a second shot, but Lucas's doctor said he was in no condition to continue, even at a shorter distance, which some accounts say was proposed. Lucas pronounced his honor satisfied, but Benton insisted on a second meeting—"a gross violation" of the *code duello* because it was the challenger, not the challenge's recipient, whose honor was at stake.

During the next six weeks, charges and countercharges were exchanged. Lucas was reluctant to pursue the matter of a second duel, but neither he nor Benton could back down gracefully enough to satisfy their notions of honor.

So, they met again on Bloody Island on a typically hot and sticky Missouri morning. This time, the men would face off at a distance of only ten feet, almost assuring that the outcome would be fatal for one of them. The count was supposed to go, "Fire, one, two, three," with the men not shooting before the count of one or after the count of three. But the second failed to say the word *fire*. Both men hesitated a beat, then shot. Lucas was hit in the side and mortally wounded, causing his shot to go wild. Benton was unhurt. At first, Lucas refused Benton's request to forgive him, but just before he died, he acquiesced, saying, "I can forgive you—I do forgive you."

Benton served as a United States senator for thirty years. Although his political fortunes were not impaired by the duel, he regretted it for the rest of his life, writing of the "pang which went through his heart when he saw the young man fall, and [that he] would have given the world to see him restored to life."

THE BIRTH OF THE WESTERN GUNFIGHT: THE HICKOK-TUTT SHOOTOUT ON THE SQUARE

In September 1865, George Ward Nichols relaxed under an awning and watched the residents of Springfield, Missouri, pass by. Before the Civil War, Nichols worked for a Boston newspaper, reporting on the events of "Bleeding Kansas." He became an aide to General John C. Frémont and later to General William T. Sherman. He was still in the army, assisting in the windup of government affairs in southwest Missouri.

Like many easterners, he regarded the inhabitants of southwest Missouri as "strange, half-civilized people" who rode mules, dressed in greasy animal skins and whose "most marked characteristic…seemed to be an indisposition to move, and their highest ambition to let their hair and beards grow." There was one man, however, who caught his eye—a man who was a little over six feet tall, with a broad chest, a gun belt with two Colt Navy revolvers strapped to his narrow waist and "a mass of fine dark hair" falling to his shoulders. His name was James Butler Hickok.

Nichols learned that Hickok, already known as "Wild Bill," had a past as colorful as his nickname. Wild Bill was involved in a shootout in Nebraska in which he killed three men while working for the Overland Stage Company. Hickok was tried for murder and acquitted on the grounds of self-defense.

HARPER'S
NEW MONTHLY MAGAZINE.

No. CCI.—FEBRUARY, 1867.—VOL. XXXIV.

WILD BILL.

SEVERAL months after the ending of the civil war I visited the city of Springfield in Southwest Missouri. Springfield is not a burgh of extensive dimensions, yet it is the largest in that part of the State, and all roads lead to it—which is one reason why it was the *point d'ap-*

VOL. XXXIV.—No. 201.—T

This article from *Harper's New Monthly Magazine* heralded James Butler "Wild Bill" Hickok as the prototypical western gunfighter. *Courtesy of the University of California.*

He left Nebraska for Missouri and became a scout and a spy for the Union army and claimed to have "sent over Jordan" a number of the enemy.

Hickok found himself in Springfield after the war with the reputation of being not only a "noted scout" but also a "desperado and gambler." In July 1865, he became acquainted with a fellow gambler named Davis Tutt, a former Confederate soldier. There was some bad blood between the two of them, which was later rumored to have been caused by "an undercurrent of a woman."

Hickok was gambling and winning from some of Tutt's friends. Tutt staked them to more money, which they promptly lost. As Hickok got up from the table, Tutt reminded him that, earlier that month, he sold him a horse for which Hickok owed forty dollars. Hickok counted out the money and paid on the spot. Not satisfied, Tutt claimed that Hickok owed him another thirty-five dollars. Hickok said, "I think you are wrong, Dave. It's only twenty-five dollars. I have a memorandum in my pocket." Suddenly, Tutt reached down and snatched Hickok's gold watch that was lying on the table. Hickok restrained himself but made it "distinctly understood," as Albert Barnitz recorded in his diary, that Tutt "couldn't walk the streets wearing his watch."

On July 21, Tutt put on the watch and his revolver, and that evening, he stepped into the street on the west side of the town square. Hickok entered from the south side, wearing his two revolvers. He told some of Tutt's friends who were loitering nearby that Tutt "shouldn't come across that square unless dead men can walk."

The two men faced each other, seventy-five yards apart. Tutt drew his gun. Hickok calmly pulled his from its holster and laid it across his left arm. The men fired simultaneously. Tutt's ball went over Hickok's head, but Hickok's struck Tutt in the chest. "Boys, I am killed," he cried. Tutt staggered and fell, dead. Hickok spun around with his gun on Tutt's friends. "Aren't you satisfied, gentlemen? Put up your shooting irons, or there'll be more dead men here." They backed off. Hickok was tried and once again acquitted, presumably on the grounds of self-defense. (The transcript of the trial was stolen.)

The story of Wild Bill's "duel" enthralled Nichols. He interviewed Hickok and got even more lurid tales from him. In January 1867, the man called Wild Bill Hickok burst on the scene in a lengthy article in *Harper's New Monthly Magazine* by Nichols. The "Wild Bill" article enjoyed the nineteenth century's equivalent of "going viral," being repeated in newspapers around the country. Hickok later confirmed that the Nichols article was only a "slight exaggeration."

Wild Bill Hickok became the first "gunfighter." His "duel" with Dave Tutt on the Springfield town square—two men facing each other, ready to "slap leather" in *mano a mano* combat from which only one would emerge—became the template for countless gunfights in dime novels, books, movies and television shows.

2.

THE UNSOLVED MURDER OF WILLIAM OWENS

Murder can have many consequences—and not only for the persons killed. In at least one case, murder led to a delay in the founding of a town.

William Owens was born into a prominent and wealthy family in Kentucky in 1796. He was the eldest son in a family that valued education so much that his father founded a school to ensure that not only his children but those from the neighborhood would have opportunities to learn. After he married Lucinda Young Cowherd in 1815 (or perhaps 1817), they set out on the adventure of settling new lands together in Franklin County, Missouri Territory. William, as the eldest son, was first in line to inherit his father's lands, but he wasn't content to wait for his father to die—not when there were lands and opportunity waiting in the West for those willing to take on the challenge.

Owens was a forward-thinking man. When he arrived in the territory, he settled in Newport, but he soon moved to the Union area. He worked as a shopkeeper and lawyer until he was appointed postmaster, then the first clerk of the Franklin County Court. Once the steamboat *Independence* made the trip from St. Louis to New Franklin in 1819, he determined that the Missouri River would soon become an important highway through the state to transport goods and people and that ports would be needed to land those goods and people. He first purchased acres of land upriver from what would become the town of Washington, and he attempted and failed to sell lots at that location. In 1831, Owens purchased acreage around a natural landing

William Owens initiated the formation of the town of Washington, Missouri, but was murdered before the idea came to fruition. His suspected murderers escaped, and although the crime has been attributed to some individuals, the murder is classified as unsolved, as no one was prosecuted. *Courtesy of the Washington, Missouri Historical Society.*

known as Washington Landing, and that would eventually form the nucleus of the town of Washington. Owens had the town surveyed and platted, ready to sell lots before tragedy struck.

John J. Porter was a deputy county clerk serving under William Owens. Porter's father followed his son into Franklin County and bought a farm. Porter believed that the farm should be titled in his name along with his father's name, but Porter Sr. refused. When Porter Sr. died, Porter produced a deed with his name listed as the owner of the farm. The deed was examined and found to be forged. The "J." in "John J. Porter" was in different handwriting and ink than the rest of the deed. Porter was indicted, and Owens was to be the chief witness against him. He was also scheduled as a witness in a case against a political enemy, Joseph McCoy, for a "grave offense."

On November 16, 1834, William Owens traveled from his home in Union to Washington on business, accompanied by John Trustell. After a long day, Owens told Trustell to proceed home and that he would soon follow. Trustell set out, and on his way to Union, he saw a man with a gun waiting in the woods. He thought he recognized the man to be a Mr. Jones, who was believed to be an army deserter, but he thought nothing of it. People carried guns and hunted in the woods every day. Trustell stopped to wait for Owens at a farm along the way. While he was there, he heard a gunshot, but again, he figured it was a hunter. When Owens failed to show, Trustell grew worried and retraced his route. He found Owens, lying in the mud, his mule nearby. Owens had been shot in the back.

Porter and McCoy were the obvious suspects. Each had a reason to want Owens dead. Reinforcing his guilt, when Porter heard that the constable was on his way, he barricaded himself in his house. He threatened to shoot anyone who came near. However, when the constable and an armed posse appeared, he surrendered.

Porter, McCoy and two additional enemies of William Owens were indicted for the murder, but they were allowed to post bond. None of the men showed up for trial, and all escaped conviction. The murder is considered unsolved.

Why didn't Lucinda immediately proceed with William's plans to file a plat and create the town of Washington, Missouri? Because in the method Owens used to sell land—contracts for deed—the purchaser only received a clear title after the full purchase price had been paid. Women did not automatically inherit property at the time, meaning the land titles were very tangled. Lucinda both sold and purchased the fifty acres from her husband's estate that became downtown Washington. Finally, on May 29, 1839, Lucinda Owens had a clear title to the land and filed the plat for the town of Washington, Missouri, accomplishing her husband's goal.

3.

"A MOST VIOLENT ACT"

The Murder of Robert Newsom and the Execution of Celia, His Slave

To all outward appearances, Robert Newsom was a solid citizen of Callaway County. He settled there in 1822 on an eight-hundred-acre farm about ten miles south of what would become the town of Fulton. He grew corn, wheat, rye and oats. By 1850, he owned five slaves. His son Harry had a farm nearby. His daughter Virginia Waynescot and her four children lived with Newsom. (Apparently, she was a widow.) Virginia served as the mistress of the household because Newsom's wife had died in 1849.

Rather than remarry, Newsom sought sexual gratification elsewhere. In 1850, he decided to buy a female slave. Newsom found a fourteen-year-old girl named Celia in Audrain County. When he returned with Celia to the family farm, Newsom raped her. Historian Melton A. McLaurin speculates (with good reason) that Newsom felt no guilt over this act because, first, it was not uncommon—and even accepted—in the slaveholding society of the nineteenth century and, second, because he repeated the act several times.

Celia was ostensibly a domestic worker in the household, but she principally served as Newsom's concubine. She gave birth to two children—likely Newsom's. He provided her a brick cabin with a large fireplace about fifty yards from the main house in a grove of cherry and pear trees. By 1855, Celia began a relationship with another of Newsom's slaves, a man named George.

Celia became pregnant in February or March 1855. The identity of the child's father is unknown. Perhaps it was George, or perhaps it was another of Newsom's children. That spring, George insisted that Celia break off her

A typical brick Missouri slave cabin, similar to the one built for Celia by Robert Newsom. *Courtesy of the Library of Congress.*

sexual relationship with Newsom because "he would have nothing to do with her if she did not quit the old man." George lacked the power to protect Celia, and he would likely be sent away or even killed if he tried. Celia was equally powerless. She begged Virginia to get her father to leave her alone because she was pregnant and sick. We don't know whether Virginia tried to intervene, but if she did, it did no good.

On June 23, 1855, Celia confronted Newsom and asked that he leave her alone. Newsom refused and told her that "he was coming to her cabin that night." Celia told him not to come and said that if he came, she "would hurt him." Around 10:00 p.m. that night, Newsom appeared at Celia's door. He came in the cabin and demanded that she have sex with him. While Newsom was speaking, Celia grabbed a large stick, "about as large as the upper side of a Windsor chair," and struck Newsom on the side of the head. He fell and threw his hands up. Celia brought the stick down on his head the second time. Newsom was dead.

Celia left the body on the floor for about an hour while she thought about what she should do next. She feared—and rightfully so—that she would be hanged. She finally decided to burn Newsom's corpse and dragged the body to the fireplace. She had to double it up to fit on the hearth. Celia set the body ablaze with some barrel staves from the yard. By daybreak, Newsom's remains had been reduced to ashes and bones. She buried some of the bones under the hearth, and she buried the remaining ashes and bone fragments near a path that led from her cabin to the stable.

The next morning, Newsom's family realized he was gone and frantically looked for him. Celia saw one of Virginia's children, eleven-year-old Coffee Waynescot, playing in a cherry tree. She offered him two dozen walnuts to empty the ashes from her fireplace. Coffee carried out his good deed, not realizing what they were, and he dumped them along the same path.

By 10:00 a.m., Harry Newsom and a neighbor, William Powell, joined in the search for Newsom. Most likely, the family was aware of George's relationship with Celia, because suspicion fell on him immediately. From his interrogation of George, Powell deduced that Celia knew what happened to Newsom. She denied it. Powell later testified, "I told her that it would be better for her to tell—that her children would not be taken away from her if she would tell and that I had a rope fashioned for her if she would not tell." At first, Celia still refused to talk, probably realizing that Powell was lying about what would happen to her children but was telling the truth about the rope. After further threats, she finally broke down and confessed. Celia said she only threatened to hurt Newsom if he did not cease his sexual demands, but she did not intend to kill him.

The searchers found Newsom's ashes and bones along the path. Virginia recovered the bones and ashes from the hearth, as well as lumps of charred flesh or internal organs, and calmly placed them in a box. Celia was taken to jail and charged with murder.

The *Missouri Republican* reported that "a most violent act was committed on the person of Robert Newsom." Although the newspaper got the place of the killing wrong, saying it occurred in Newsom's kitchen, the other details were essentially correct. The correspondent described the killing as being "committed without any apparent cause," thus omitting the justification given in Celia's statements. Indeed, when the *St. Louis Globe-Democrat* published a lengthy article about the killing and included her confession, it also failed to mention that Newsom had raped her when she was fourteen, fathered children by her and had gone to her cabin that night, intent on forcing her to have sex with him.

While Celia was in jail awaiting trial, the authorities sent Jefferson Jones, a wealthy lawyer, to interrogate her. No one believed that Celia, a nineteen-year-old pregnant woman, could have acted alone in killing Newsom and disposing of his body. Three times, Jones demanded to know whether George was involved, and three times, Celia said he was never there and knew nothing about Newsom's death or the burning and disposal of his remains. George, however, could see that suspicion was falling heavily on him. He ran away.

Judge William A. Hall appointed three attorneys to represent Celia. The lead counsel was John Jameson. Jameson practiced law in Callaway County for thirty years. He served three terms in Congress, and at one time, he was the speaker of the Missouri General Assembly. The two other lawyers, Nathan Kouns and Isaac Boulware, were in their twenties. Hall probably appointed them for their abilities to assist Jameson with legal research because neither was experienced.

The trial began in Fulton on October 9, 1855. Jameson's plan was to argue that Celia acted to prevent her rape, a defense afforded by Missouri law to "any woman." Certainly, the law applied to white women, but did it apply to an enslaved Black woman?

The prosecution called Jefferson Jones to recount his interview with Celia in early July. Jones said that Celia told him she struck the second blow to Newsom's head "because he had approached." When Jameson had his chance, he immediately got Jones to say that Celia told him that "the old man had sexual intercourse with her." He asked whether it was true that Newsom raped her right after he bought her. Jones equivocated, saying only that he couldn't "positively say whether Celia said the deceased forced her on the way home from Audrain County. I have heard that he did, but do not know with certainty whether she told me so."

The prosecution only asked William Powell about finding Newsom's bones. Jameson brought out Powell's interrogation of Celia and his threats against her children and of the "rope fashioned for her." Jameson asked six times about the threats Celia made to hurt Newsom—not to kill him, but to hurt him—if he did not leave her alone. Celia, Powell conceded, said "she did not want to kill him, struck him but did not want to kill." The final witness, Thomas Shoatman, had accompanied Jones in his interview of Celia. He said that the "reason she gave for striking him a second time was that he threw his hands up," suggesting that Newsom made some menacing move that justified the second blow. Celia did not testify at the trial because, under the common law at that time, criminal defendants, white or Black, free or enslaved, were not allowed to testify on their own behalf. (Missouri changed this rule by statute in 1877.)

Judge Hall instructed the jury to find Celia guilty of first-degree murder if she acted deliberately and premeditatedly in killing Newsom. The deliberation necessary "need be but for a moment before the killing." (This is still the standard today, with prosecutors sometimes emphasizing the point by snapping their finger and saying it takes no longer than that.) Judge Hall told the jury there was no evidence of self-defense and specifically instructed the jury that it was no defense that Newsom had come to Celia's cabin with the aim of having sex with her. He rejected Jameson's request that the jury be instructed to acquit Celia if she killed Newsom "to prevent him from forcing her to sexual intercourse." Jameson argued that the Missouri statute afforded a defense to "any woman" who killed a man who was trying to rape her "embraces slave women as well as white women." The judge rejected this proposition—it was, as McLaurin points out, a radical threat to a slave society—thus upholding the principle that a white slaveowner could rape his enslaved women with impunity.

Needless to say, with these instructions, the jury found Celia guilty of murder in the first degree. Judge Hall sentenced her to be hanged on November 16. Jameson's motion for a new trial was denied, and he sought to stay the execution, pending an appeal to the Missouri Supreme Court. Hall denied the stay. At that time, the Supreme Court had to grant permission for an appeal to be heard, even in a murder case. As the date of Celia's execution drew near, she escaped on November 11, or as her lawyers put it, she was "taken out by someone" just long enough to have the execution date pass. Hall set a new date: December 21. Jameson asked Supreme Court judge Abiel Leonard for a stay of the execution so that her appeal could be taken up by the court in January, writing that "the greater portion of the community" in Callaway County was "much interested in her behalf." Leonard refused, however, holding that there was no probable cause that such an appeal would be successful.

Celia was hanged in Fulton, Missouri, on December 21, 1855. The place of her burial and what happened to her children is unknown.

4.

"THE DIRTY LITTLE COWARD WHO SHOT MR. HOWARD LAID POOR JESSE IN HIS GRAVE"

Jesse James

After Mark Twain and Harry Truman—and maybe even ahead of them—Jesse James is one of the most famous Missourians ever. He has played many roles in our culture: Civil War guerrilla, bank and train robber, killer, Robin Hood type, political icon, dime-novel hero, movie and television star. His story is encrusted with so many myths that it is sometimes difficult to sort out the truth from the fiction. Even his serious biographers disagree about important aspects of his life, some of them in the literary equivalent of Wild West shootouts.

Jesse Woodson James was born to Robert James and Zerelda Cole James on September 5, 1847, in Clay County, Missouri. Robert was a college-educated (he had a bachelor's and master's degree), fire-breathing minister from Kentucky. He married the equally fire-breathing and college-educated Zerelda in 1841. They had an older son, Franklin, in 1843, and a daughter, Susan, in 1849. Robert followed the gold rush to California to save miners' souls and perhaps pick up some wealth for his family—although, not necessarily in that order. Unfortunately, he died from disease in a mining camp in 1850.

Zerelda married twice after that; she had an unhappy and mercifully short union with Benjamin Simms and a much more satisfying and long-lived marriage to Reuben Samuel. They lived what today we would call a solid, middle-class life, raising tobacco, corn and other products on their farm with the help of six or seven slaves. Then, the war came.

Jesse James. *Courtesy of the Library of Congress.*

Eighteen-year-old Frank joined the Missouri State Guard and fought against Union troops at the Battles of Wilson's Creek and Lexington. He fell ill and left the army, returning home in late 1861. Frank stayed away from the war until May 1863, when he joined some local guerrillas. Jesse wanted to become a guerrilla like his brother, but Zerelda refused to let him go until 1864. Jesse and Frank became members of a band led by William Anderson, better known as "Bloody Bill." In the fall of 1864, Frank left Missouri with William Quantrill to carry out guerrilla activities in Kentucky. Jesse stayed in Missouri until Anderson was killed by Missouri militiamen led by Samuel Cox. He spent the winter of 1864–65 in Texas, resuming his Missouri guerrilla activities in early 1865.

On May 8, Jesse and his good friend Arch Clement murdered ten men in Kingsville. A week later, Jesse and Clement were surprised by a patrol of Wisconsin cavalry. Jesse claimed that he was going to surrender and seek amnesty, although we only have his word for that. Jesse was shot in the chest. While recuperating in Lexington, he signed the loyalty oath required for amnesty. He was later taken to Harlem, Missouri (now North Kansas City), for a lengthy convalescence. His nurse was his cousin, Zerelda "Zee" Mimms. Thus began a courtship that resulted in marriage nine years later.

Exactly how long Jesse was laid up by this gunshot wound is disputed by his biographers. Some say that Jesse was so weakened that he could not do much for nearly four years. We do know he traveled to Tennessee and may have traveled to California to recuperate. Others claim he was not nearly so bad off.

Jesse's biographers also disagree on how many and which robberies he participated in. Jesse and Frank may have robbed as many as twenty-five banks and trains together (Frank worked some robberies without Jesse and vice versa), but probably the number is closer to fifteen. A gang of about a dozen former Confederate guerrillas, most likely including Frank, carried out the first peacetime bank robbery in Liberty, Missouri, on February 14, 1866. Jesse is sometimes identified as the mastermind behind this robbery, but that is unlikely because he was only eighteen at the time.

The first robbery that everyone agrees Jesse took part in was that of the Gallatin Bank on December 7, 1869. Two men entered the bank and shot the cashier, John Sheets, in cold blood, supposedly because they mistook him for Samuel Cox, the owner of the bank and the man who led the troops that killed Bloody Bill Anderson. Jesse was recognized by the horse he rode, although Zerelda said that Jesse had sold it a couple weeks earlier and that he was home at the time of the robbery (an alibi she would repeat for other robberies). Frank and Jesse were hardly household names yet. The newspapers identified the robbers as "two brothers by the name of James." A posse later came to the Samuel farm, but the brothers escaped.

The James gang expanded its horizons to other states, robbing banks in Iowa and Kentucky, killing the cashier at the latter. The posses that chased them were ineffectual. In September 1872, Frank, Jesse and Cole Younger pulled off an especially daring robbery of the Kansas City Fair. Three men rode up to the ticket booth in the afternoon as hundreds of persons left the event. The masked robbers took $978 from the till but became involved in a tussle with a guy named Ben Wallace, who was in charge of the money. The James brothers got away once again. Wallace would hardly be remembered but for the fact that his granddaughter Bess married a man from Independence who later became president of the United States—Harry Truman.

After the Gallatin and Kansas City Fair robberies, Jesse wrote letters to newspapers criticizing the Radical Republican state government and the administration of President Ulysses Grant. James's biographers believe that the letters were written by—or at least extensively edited by—newspaperman John Newman Edwards. Edwards was a former Confederate officer and rabidly anti-Republican Democrat. T.J. Stiles credited Edwards with going a long way in making Jesse James a political symbol and "the last rebel of the Civil War." Edwards himself wrote an editorial about the Kansas City caper titled "The Chivalry of Crime"; it glorified the robbers as men of "stupendous nerve and fearlessness."

Around 3:00 p.m. on the afternoon of January 31, 1874, five men rode into the tiny town of Gads Hill, Missouri, consisting of three houses and a railroad station about one hundred miles south of St. Louis. They robbed the citizens and then herded them into the station. A couple hours later, the southbound *Little Rock Express* pulled into sight. One of the men flagged it down. When the conductor stepped off the train to see what was going on, a masked man put a revolver in his face and shouted, "Stand still or I'll blow the top of your damned head off!"

The gang proceeded to rummage through the baggage car, taking $1,080 from the Adams Express Company safe and leaving a receipt that read "Robbed at Gads Hill." They then moved through the passenger cars, relieving the passengers of money and jewelry. One of the robbers, possibly Frank, supposedly quoted Shakespeare. (If true, this may have been an homage to *Henry IV, Part One*, in which Falstaff commits a robbery at Gads Hill and is in turn robbed by Prince Hal.) Before the robbers left, one of them gave a passenger a telegram to be sent to the *St. Louis Post-Dispatch* that began, "The most daring train robbery on record." The gang rode away, and of course, a hastily gathered posse couldn't track them down.

The Gads Hill Robbery—the first train robbery in Missouri—was bloodless. But bloodshed would follow directly from it. The Pinkerton Detective Agency was owned by Allan Pinkerton, who had served for a time as General George McClellan's spymaster during the Civil War, supplying him with the erroneous information he craved that inflated the number of General Robert E. Lee's army to levels that justified inaction. Pinkerton suffered no loss of reputation, except among historians. The express company that was the victim of the Gads Hill Robbery hired his agency to find the James brothers and bring them to justice.

After a long search, during which one of its agents, Joseph Whicher, was murdered by Jesse and a couple of henchmen, the agency thought it had the James brothers trapped. A local informant told them the James boys would be at the Samuel farm the night of January 25, 1875. They were there but left before seven Pinkerton men closed in. The Pinkertons surrounded the house and threw firebombs inside. One rolled inside the fireplace. Reuben managed to get it out, but it exploded, mortally wounding Jesse's nine-year-old half-brother Archie and shattering Zerelda's right wrist. (Her hand had to be amputated.)

Jesse and Frank vowed revenge. They tracked down the informant and murdered him. Whether they killed the right man is disputed. And it is likely that it was Frank who did the shooting. Old-timers said, "Frank was the cold-bloodest of the two. If he said he would kill ya, he would kill you, but you could talk Jesse out of it." A lawyer who cooperated with the Pinkertons got the message and left for Minnesota. None of the Pinkerton men were ever brought to trial for the attack.

Frank and Jesse left Missouri for a time. Frank led the gang in a robbery of a bank in Huntington, West Virginia. Jesse, it seems, took time off to spend with his new bride. He and Zee were married the year before and settled in Nashville, Tennessee, as Mr. and Mrs. Howard, using the proceeds from his robberies to buy a house.

On July 7, 1876, Jesse, Frank, Cole and Bob Younger, Clell Miller, Charlie Pitts, Bill Chadwell and Hobbs Kerry robbed a Missouri Pacific train near the crossing of the Lamine River at a place known locally as Rocky Cut. The robbers piled railroad ties on the track and flagged down the train. A minister prayed and led songs while the passengers wailed and cried out. The gang rifled the Adams Express Company safe and ended up taking an estimated $15,000 in cash and bonds. The usual ineffective posse was mounted. It unfortunately killed an innocent woman in a shooting accident, but it did finally manage to capture Hobbs Kerry a few days later.

The same gang that executed the Rocky Cut Robbery, plus Jim Younger and minus Hobbs Kerry, decided to go to a place they believed did not know how to handle a brazen robbery and where no one would ever expect them. They could not have been more wrong.

On September 7, 1876, five men rode into Northfield, Minnesota, to the First National Bank. Three of them (accounts differ, but it was probably Frank, Bob Younger and Charlie Pitts) went inside the bank. Two others, probably Cole Younger and Clell Miller, stayed outside. A couple blocks away Jesse, Jim Younger and Bill Chadwell waited to guard the planned escape route. Things went awry quickly. Frank brandished his revolver and yelled, "Throw up your hands, for we intend to rob this bank, and if you holler, we will blow your God damned brains out!" Outside, Henry Wheeler, a University of Michigan medical student who was home on break, realized what was happening and ran down the street, shouting, "Robbery! They are robbing the bank!" Citizens grabbed guns, and soon, the street was full of gunfire. Jesse and his companions rushed to the aid of Frank and the others. Wheeler grabbed a rifle and shot Miller dead from a building across the street. Another citizen killed Chadwell. Cole Younger took a bullet to his hip. Inside, Frank demanded that the cashier, Joseph Heywood, open the safe. Heywood said it was on a time lock. Frank pistol-whipped him, and right before he left, he put his revolver to Heywood's head and pulled the trigger. Heywood lay dead. Frank scooped up the money from the cash drawer and bolted outside. The surviving six fought their way out of town. The total take from the robbery: $26.70.

This time, the posse was persistent, if not always competent. Jesse and Frank split from the Younger brothers and Pitts after a few days. The James brothers made their way back to Missouri after a lengthy and circuitous trip. Shortly afterward, Frank and Jesse returned to Tennessee. The posse, however, caught up with the others. Charlie Pitts was killed in a final gun battle. The Younger brothers surrendered and were convicted of murder.

(Wheeler ended up with Clell Miller's body, and Miller's skeleton hung in the doctor's office for years.)

Frank was tired of running from the law and took up life as a law-abiding man named Woodson. Jesse grew restless and rounded up a new gang. On October 7, 1879, Jesse struck again. Five men stopped an eastbound train at Glendale, near Independence, Missouri. They rifled the express car and stuffed a bag full of what they believed was $60,000 in paper currency. It turned out to be mostly nonnegotiable securities, but there was $6,000 in cash to split among the gang. One of the gang members was Ed Miller, the brother of Clell who was killed in the Northfield robbery. The exact circumstances of his death aren't known, but shortly after the Glendale robbery, Jesse and Ed apparently had an argument, and Jesse killed him.

Frank was back on the outlaw trail with Jesse in early 1881. Jesse, Frank and a couple of others knocked over a federal payroll for workers on the Muscle Shoals Canal in northern Alabama. They got $5,200 in currency and coin. Things were becoming too hot in Tennessee for the brothers, and they returned to their home state of Missouri for their final two robberies.

Jesse planned several robberies, but most of them were scrubbed for various reasons. In July 1881, however, Jesse decided to rob a Rock Island train. Jesse, along with Frank, their cousins Clarence and Wood Hite and Dick Liddil, boarded the train at Winston, a few miles southwest of Gallatin, the site of their first bank robbery. Jesse, Frank and Wood went to the smoking car, while Clarence and Liddil stationed themselves outside the baggage car. When the train pulled away, Jesse and the other two robbers banged into the car, shouting, "Hands up!" The conductor, William Westfall, made some sort of motion that Jesse interpreted as going for a gun. Jesse shot and killed him. During the confusion, passenger Frank McMillan ducked out of the car and crouched outside the door along with another man. McMillan stood up to take a peek at the ongoing robbery inside when a bullet fired by one of the robbers struck him in the head. McMillan fell dead. The gang forced the express agent to open the safe. Instead of finding several thousand dollars, as they expected, the robbers only found about $700 in cash. The gang mounted horses they had hidden nearby and, as usual, eluded the posse.

The Winston robbery created a political stir, with Republican papers claiming that the Democrats were shielding the James gang. Missouri's governor Thomas T. Crittenden met with a delegation of railroad and express company executives to solicit their support—and cash—for a reward. Crittenden issued a proclamation that said anyone who provided information for the arrest of Jesse and Frank James would receive $10,000, plus another $10,000 if the brothers were convicted of either the Glendale or Winston robberies—or both.

Jesse and Frank's final robbery together took place on September 7, 1881. A local boy from Ray County, Charlie Ford, was added to the crew that had pulled off the Winston robbery. About a mile from where Jesse and Frank robbed the Glendale train, the railroad entered a curve through a deep cut known as Blue Cut. The gang piled rocks and ties on the track, and a person waving a red lantern flagged down the train as it came around the curve. Wood Hite and Ford broke into the express car and forced the messenger to open the safe. Ford encouraged him to move a little quicker by striking him on the head with his revolver. When the safe proved to have only about $400, Ford gave the messenger another blow. In the meantime, Jesse, Frank, Clarence Hite and Liddil went through the passenger cars, relieving the men and women there of their money and jewelry. The usual posse chased after the gang with usual result—they got away.

Jesse went to live in St. Joseph, Missouri, under the alias of Thomas Howard. It is said that his son, Jesse Edward James (not Jesse Jr., as he is sometimes called), didn't even know his true name at the time. He thought his name was Tim Howard. In the meantime, Charlie Ford and his brother Bob got mixed up with the Hite family and their dispute with Dick Liddil, which resulted in a gun battle in December 1881, during which Bob Ford shot Wood Hite in the head. Rumors about Jesse's killing of Ed Miller after the Glendale robbery sparked fears that Jesse would take revenge on whoever killed his cousin Wood when he found out about it.

Bob Ford, described as "the dirty little coward who shot Mr. Howard" in the "Ballad of Jesse James," a "song that was made by Billy Gashade as soon as the word did arrive." *Courtesy of the Library of Congress.*

On January 13, 1882, Bob Ford met with Governor Crittenden and Sheriff Henry Timberlake at a hotel in Kansas City. Bob claimed that he was told the reward was for bringing in Jesse and Frank "dead or alive," but Crittenden (and Charlie) said it was only for the capture and conviction of the two outlaws.

On April 3, Jesse prepared to leave St. Joseph with Charlie and Bob Ford to rob a bank in Platte City, Missouri. It was a

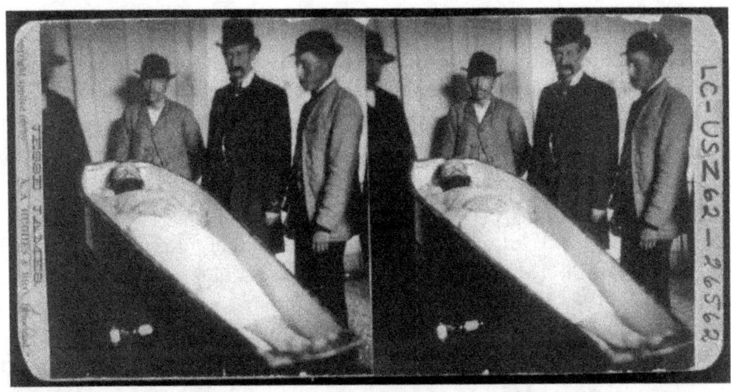

Jesse James's body on display in its coffin, April 1882. Note the scar on his right upper chest from a bullet wound he suffered in 1865. *Courtesy of the Library of Congress.*

warm day. Jesse took off his coat and threw his gun belt on a nearby chair. He noticed that a picture of his favorite racehorse was crooked and dusty. He went to fix it. Charlie later testified, "When he turned his back, I gave my brother the wink, and we both pulled our pistols, but he, my brother, was a little the quickest and fired first....He heard us cock our pistols and [was about] to turn his head. The ball hit him in the back of the head and he fell."

The Ford brothers sent a telegram to Governor Crittenden and surrendered to the city marshal. Both pleaded guilty on the morning of April 17, and Governor Crittenden pardoned them in the afternoon. Crittenden said he was "not regretful of his death." The *St. Louis Republican* noted that the journals that called for Jesse's arrest were then "engaging in maudlin sentimentality over the manner of his death." Jesse's body was displayed and photographed at the funeral parlor. Souvenir hunters struggled over who could take what relics. Jesse was buried on his family's farm. (His body was disinterred and reburied in Kearny, Missouri, in 1902.)

Charlie and Bob Ford—"the dirty little coward who shot Mr. Howard laid poor Jesse in his grave"—reenacted the shooting more than eight hundred times on the stage, but neither of their lives ended peacefully. Charlie committed suicide in 1884. Bob was murdered in a Colorado saloon in 1892.

Frank took the opportunity of the uproar over Jesse's death to give up his life of crime. In a meeting that was likely orchestrated by John Newman Edwards, Frank went to the Governor's Mansion in Jefferson City, dramatically turned over his revolver to Governor Crittenden and agreed to stand trial for the Winston murders—but only on the condition that he not be extradited to Minnesota for killing Joseph Heywood.

Frank evidently hoped for a more sympathetic jury in Missouri, and he was not disappointed. Frank mustered a nineteenth-century legal dream team headed by John F. Philips (Crittenden's commanding officer in the Union army) and former lieutenant governor Charles P. Johnson. After sixteen days of trial, the jury acquitted Frank. Frank was later tried and also acquitted of the Muscle Shoals robbery. He was never convicted of any crime. Frank drifted among various jobs after his acquittals, including acting as a doorman for a burlesque theater in St. Louis and as a character in a Wild West show. He died in 1915.

Jesse died in 1882, but his memory lived on. He was lionized in songs, dime novels, movies and television shows. The "Ballad of Jesse James," which supposedly, as the song says, "was made by Billy Gashade as soon as the news did arrive," has been recorded numerous times by artists ranging from Carl Sandburg to Bruce Springsteen. Jesse's son starred as his father in two movies shot in Missouri in the 1920s. *Jesse James*, starring Tyrone Power and Henry Fonda, was the third-highest-grossing picture of 1939 after *Gone with the Wind* and *The Wizard of Oz*. Another Missourian, Brad Pitt, played Jesse in the 2007 movie *The Assassination of Jesse James by the Coward Robert Ford.*

There have been many claims that Jesse wasn't killed in April 1882. Jesse's remains were exhumed in 1995. A DNA analysis proved that the man who had laid in the grave for more than one hundred years was not just Mr. Howard but was indeed Jesse James.

Why was Jesse James so popular? Perhaps it was best put by English writer Oscar Wilde, who happened to be in St. Joseph a couple of weeks after Jesse was killed. "The Americans," he said, "are certainly great hero-worshippers and always take their heroes from the criminal classes."

5.

MURDER, MUSIC AND MOVIES

Within the span of four years and the space of a few blocks in downtown St. Louis, two murders occurred that spawned songs that have been recorded hundreds of times in dozens of versions. And while many movies have been filmed in St. Louis, only one was shot in the very location where the story originally occurred.

"TWO MEN WHO GAMBLED LATE": STAGGER LEE AND BILLY

The night may have been clear and the moon may have been yellow (as the Lloyd Price song goes), but it is likely that neither Lee "Stack Lee" Shelton nor William "Billy" Lyons noticed.

On Christmas night in 1895, Billy and his friend Henry Crump were enjoying a beer in the Bill Curtis Saloon. The crowd quieted as they looked toward the door. There was Stack Lee, dressed in the dandified style of a St. Louis "mack" or pimp. There was an undercurrent of trouble between Billy and Stack Lee. Billy's stepbrother had killed a friend of Lee's a few months before, and Lee had supposedly sworn to take revenge against the family. But this night began on a friendly note. Lee asked, "Who's treating?" Billy offered Lee a drink, and they chatted for a time.

The talk turned to politics, and then, it turned into argument. Lee hit Billy's derby bowler, denting it. Billy snatched Lee's brand-new Stetson hat off his head. A witness later testified that Lee said, "Give me my hat." And

Billy said, "I ain't going to give it to you. I want pay for this," indicating his damaged bowler.

Lee asked, "How much do you want?"

Billy said, "I want six bits."

Lee snorted and said, "Six bits will buy a box of those hats."

Then, Lee took his .44 pistol out of his pocket and said, "If you don't give me my hat, I will blow your brains out." Billy replied, "I am not going to give you the hat. You can kill me." And Lee proceeded to do just that. He shot Billy in the abdomen. Billy staggered and fell to the floor. Lee bent over and said, "I told you to give me my hat." Lee then picked up his Stetson, slapped it on his head and walked out the door. Billy died a few hours later.

For many years, people thought Stagger Lee or Stack Lee or Stagolee (all of these names appear in the various versions of the song) and Billy weren't real people. They were. Billy Lyons was thirty-one years old when he died. He was listed in the city directory as a watchman and left three children behind. He was connected to a powerful Republican political faction through the marriage of his sister to Henry Bridgewater, a prominent African American politician who was reputed to be the richest Black person in town. Lee Shelton, who was thirty years old at the time, was aligned with the emerging Black Democratic organizations that opposed the Bridgewater outfit. He was the president of a political and social organization called the Colored Four Hundred Club. At the time of the shooting, he was the proprietor of the Modern Horseshoe Club, which was one of the prestigious centers of jazz and blues music. It was, however, also known as a "lid club," an ostensibly legitimate drinking and music establishment that provided a cover for gambling and prostitution.

Shelton was arrested early the next morning, around the time Lyons died. The police took Shelton to the Four Courts building and charged him with first-degree murder. Theodore Dreiser, who was then a young crime reporter for the *St. Louis Globe-Democrat*, described the Four Courts as a place with a "more dismal atmosphere that…would be hard to find." It had "the city detention wards, the office of the district attorney, the chief of police, the chief of detectives, the city attorney and a 'reporters' room." Its inhabitants included "harlots, criminals, murderers, buzzard lawyers, political judges, detectives, police agents, and court officials, generally—what a company!"

Shelton, not a man without means, hired Nat Dryden to represent him. Dryden was one of the best criminal lawyers in the state, although even his friends thought him "eccentric." Part of his eccentricity was no doubt due to his drug and alcohol habit, but in the courtroom, he was a bulldog.

Above: Stagger Lee's "lid club" as it appears today. *Photograph by køpper from STL, USA.*

Left: The Four Courts building housed the jail, courtrooms, police and prosecutors' offices and was adjacent to the city morgue. It was demolished in 1927. *Courtesy of the Missouri Historical Society.*

After one delay, due to some missing prosecution witnesses (the rumor was they had been paid to leave town), Shelton was finally brought to trial on July 15, 1896. Dryden argued that Shelton shot Lyons in self-defense. The jury deliberated for twenty-two hours but could not agree on a verdict. Shelton was released on bail, pending a second trial.

Dryden wasn't around for Shelton's second trial in May 1897. He had possibly fallen ill, as he died three months later. Shelton's new lead attorney, Charles P. Johnson, was no slouch. He was a former lieutenant governor of Missouri, a leading criminal lawyer in the state and a professor of criminal law at the Washington University of St. Louis Law School. Fifteen years earlier, Johnson had been part of the legal team that helped Frank James beat a murder charge.

Things were relatively uneventful for a murder trial, until the prosecution called Henry Crump to the witness stand. Crump began to testify about how he had given Billy Lyons a knife and that Billy had pulled it on Stack Lee. The prosecutor reached into his pile of papers and took out a statement that Crump had given prior to the first trial, in which he said Lyons was unarmed. Johnson objected, which led to an argument, and this led to the two lawyers nearly coming to blows. They only separated when the bailiff stepped between them. Tempers cooled, Johnson's objection was sustained and Crump was allowed to testify about the knife. Alas, it did no good for Shelton. The jury found him guilty of second-degree murder, saving Shelton from the gallows. Instead, he was sentenced to twenty-five years in prison. Shelton was paroled in 1909 but found himself back in prison two years later for pistol-whipping a man over a debt. He died in 1911. By then, the legend of Stagger Lee and Billy had firmly taken hold in the African American community from St. Louis to the mouth of the Mississippi.

The origin of the ballad of Stack Lee or Stagolee or Stagger Lee isn't known. A good guess of its source might be in the clubs of "Chestnut Valley" or one of the other red-light districts of the city. The origin of Lee Shelton's nickname, which morphed into various versions as the song made its way up and down the river, isn't known either. Maybe he worked for a steamboat known as the *Stack Lee* that was supposedly well-known for its prostitutes. He may have been called "Stag" Lee because he threw stag parties for "sporting men."

Whatever the answer to these questions, the song grew in popularity, as it was sung by Black roustabouts on the levee and then in the cotton fields and even the prisons of the Deep South. The "Stagger Lee Blues" was first recorded in 1923 by—of all persons—Fred Waring and the Pennsylvanians as a jazz instrumental. The classic early version with lyrics was recorded by Mississippi John Hurt in 1928. Since that time, one version or another of "Stagger Lee" has been recorded by more than four hundred artists in numerous genres ranging from Pat Boone and Wilson Pickett to the Grateful Dead. The best-known modern version is Lloyd Price's hit that reached number one on the charts in 1959.

"A NEW MAN'S FACE IN HELL": FRANKIE AND JOHNNY

The big stories on the front pages of the October 16, 1899 editions of the *St. Louis Post-Dispatch* and the *St. Louis Globe-Democrat* were the America's Cup Race (the American entry defeated Irish tea baron Sir Thomas Lipton)

Frankie Baker, circa 1899. *Courtesy of the St. Louis Mercantile Library at the University of Missouri–St. Louis.*

and the Boer War in South Africa. In a brief note, the *Post-Dispatch* reported that Frankie Backer had shot Allen Britt in the abdomen. Buried on the last page of the *Globe* was a slightly longer story that also recounted the shooting of Allen Britt by Frankie Backer. There was nothing in the papers to suggest that the incident would become the seed for an unforgettable ballad that inspired movies, books and even a mural in the Missouri State Capitol.

Frankie Baker, not Backer as reported in the papers, was a beauty who dressed well with, as one of her neighbors described her, a "proud and racy bearing." Some said she was a "queen sport," or, in other words, a prostitute. Allen Britt (also known as Albert or simply Al) was seventeen years old and a talented piano player. He met Frankie at a dance and moved in with her at 212 Targee Street, "where Frankie sat for her company." Targee Street, which is now long gone (it disappeared in the 1930s, when the Municipal Auditorium, now the Stifel Theater, was built), was in the middle of a sporting area, where prostitution, gambling and drugs were prevalent.

On the evening of October 14, Allen had not come home. Frankie went searching for him and found him with Alice Pryar at the Phoenix Hotel. They quarreled and drew a crowd. Frankie went home alone. Around 3:00 a.m., Allen showed up at their Targee Street apartment. They quarreled again. Here, accounts diverge. Richard Clay, a neighbor, said that Allen threatened to leave Frankie. She began to cry and started out the door to find Alice. Allen then threatened to kill her, and that's when she grabbed a gun and fired.

According to Frankie, in a newspaper interview that she gave forty years later, Allen returned to the apartment and woke Frankie up. He grabbed a lamp and threw it at her. "Say, are you trying to get me hurt?" Frankie asked. "I am the boss here. I pay rent, and I have to protect myself." Allen reached in his pocket and pulled out a knife. Seeing this, Frankie got a revolver from under her pillow—a .41, not a .44, she was quite insistent on the point. According to the ballad:

First time she shot him, he staggered, second time she shot him, he fell
Third time she shot him, O Lordy, there was a new man's face in Hell
She killed her man who had done her wrong.

In fact, Frankie shot Allen once—and only once—in the stomach, but that was enough. Allen staggered to his mother's home down the street, where he collapsed. He lingered on at City Hospital for three days before dying on October 19.

Frankie was charged with first-degree murder, but a coroner's jury held it to be a justifiable homicide, no doubt based on self-defense. Nevertheless, she was kept in jail in the Four Courts building, pending a circuit court trial. "I ain't superstitious no more," she told a reporter years later. "Because I went to trial on Friday, November 13, 1899, and the bad luck omens didn't go against me." (Fortunately, for her peace of mind, Frankie didn't check a calendar because November 13, 1899, was a Monday.)

According to an 1899 article in the *St. Louis Palladium* by Ira Cooper (then a young reporter and later the first African American lieutenant in the St. Louis police force), on the night following the shooting, Bill Dooley, a Black pianist and songwriter, "composed a sorrowful dirge" he called "Frankie Killed Allen." We now know it as "Frankie and Johnny" because the Britt family objected vociferously to having Allen mentioned in the song. Novelist and music historian Cecil Brown also credits Dooley with composing the original "Stack Lee" ballad based on its style and the similarities between the two.

As with Stagger Lee, the ballad of Frankie and Johnny proved to be immensely popular; it was all over St. Louis within a couple of months. Frankie left St. Louis because, as she said, "I'd come out of my house, and they'd follow me down the street, just singing and singing." Frankie was so tired of hearing it "she ran to Omaha in humiliation." But Omaha was no refuge. The song had already spread throughout the country.

In 1930, John Huston, then an unknown young author, wrote a play titled *Frankie and Johnny*, which is now best forgotten. But when it was published, it included an interview with Richard Clay, for which the book is best remembered. The interview provided far more detail about the events of that night than the sparse newspaper accounts. The book also had twenty versions of the song, including the "St. Louis" version on which the play was based. A scholar later identified more than 290 versions of the ballad.

The tale of a woman who shot her man because "he done her wrong" was irresistible to Hollywood. In 1933, Paramount Pictures released *She*

Done Him Wrong, starring Mae West and Cary Grant. The movie featured the song "Frankie and Johnny," although it is better known for West's invitation to Grant: "Come up sometime and see me." Frankie Baker emerged from the shadows to sue the company for defamation. She lost, but Republic Pictures, perhaps emboldened by that legal victory, released *Frankie and Johnnie* in 1936, starring Helen Morgan and Chester Morris. The movie, in Hollywood parlance, "laid an egg," but it revived talk about Frankie and the man who done her wrong. That same year, Thomas Hart Benton, who was named for his father's great-uncle, the nineteenth-century Missouri senator and duelist, completed a mural in the Missouri State Capitol that portrayed Frankie shooting Johnny, albeit in a bar and not in a hotel room or apartment.

At the time, Frankie was living in Portland, Oregon, where she ran a shoeshine parlor. Having yet another movie based on her life was too much. She hired a lawyer in St. Louis and filed another lawsuit, claiming that the Republic picture defamed her.

Her return to St. Louis was highly anticipated, and she did not disappoint. When asked by newspapermen if she wore diamonds as big as goose eggs as

"Frankie and Johnny," from Thomas Hart Benton's mural, *A Social History of Missouri*, at the Missouri State Capitol, completed in 1936. *Courtesy of the Missouri State Archives.*

Frankie Baker, in February 1942, eating a meal while on a break from the trial against Republic Pictures in St. Louis. *Courtesy of the St. Louis Mercantile Library at the University of Missouri–St. Louis.*

some versions of the song said, she replied, "Only an average-size one." Did she buy Allen hundred-dollar suits? "Not necessarily."

The movie was shown to the jury, but most of the testimony was centered on whether Frankie was actually the subject of the ballad. Republic cited Carl Sandburg, who had written that the song originated before the Civil War. Yet another expert claimed that it was sung by Union soldiers during the siege of Vicksburg in 1863. Some locals testified that they heard it on the streets of St. Louis years before Allen was shot. Frankie's lawyer produced his own experts, who countered that the song was Bill Dooley's composition and that there was nothing to substantiate the claims of it having been in circulation earlier than 1899.

Republic's star witness was Sigmund Spaeth, dubbed "The Tune Detective" by the *Post-Dispatch*. An authority on popular songs, Spaeth had written a book years earlier in which he credited "Frankie and Johnny" to an unknown balladeer in St. Louis in the 1890s. By the time of the 1942 trial, he had changed his mind and said it was far older. As part of his testimony, Spaeth burst into song, perhaps to the astonishment of the judge and jury, about how Frankie shot Johnny "roota-toot-toot" because "he done her wrong." Spaeth pointed out that the Frankie at the trial, demurely dressed in a tan trench coat, floppy slouch hat and rubbers over her shoes, could not have been the expensively outfitted "Frankie" of the song. (Frankie was twenty-three at the time of the shooting and sixty-six at the time of the trial.)

Frankie took the stand to deny the truth of nearly everything in the song. Her answers on the witness stand were not as flippant as her newspaper interviews, but she denied being a "queen sport," said that she never wore diamonds and claimed that she never bought Allen suits.

"How many shots were fired?"

"One."

"Did you shoot him with a roota-toot-toot?"

Frankie rolled her eyes. "No, sir."

The chances of an African American woman getting justice from a white St. Louis jury against a large corporation in 1942 were probably never great. The jury deliberated for a little over an hour before returning a defense verdict, sending Frankie Baker back to Portland empty-handed, and there, she died ten years later.

They done her wrong.

THE GREAT ST. LOUIS BANK ROBBERY

On April 24, 1953, three men entered the Southwest Bank at the corner of Kingshighway and Southwest Boulevard in St. Louis. Fred Bowerman had been robbing banks and other businesses for almost twenty-five years in between stretches in prison. He had just earned a place on the FBI's Ten

Most Wanted List the month before for his robbery of a bank in South Bend, Indiana, where he took $53,000 and shot a bank employee for "raising his hands too slowly."

Bowerman's gang included three other men. Frank Vito had helped rob the South Bend bank. Vito was out on bail, charged with having participated in a $40,000 liquor hijacking in Chicago. William Scholl was a disabled veteran with a clean record. He joined Bowerman after meeting him in a bar and being promised that he would make "$5,000 in five minutes" if he helped hit the bank in St. Louis. Glenn Chernick, the "wheelman," was a young, good-looking former football player at Marquette University who was Vito's neighbor in Chicago.

The robbers spent several days "casing" the bank, noting carefully when police drove by and other details. Bowerman drew up a map and a colored chart to show the best times to rob the bank—green for the good hours and red for the bad. They met in nearby Tower Grove Park each day to go over the plans. Bowerman finally decided that the best time was mid-morning on a Friday because the bank would have payroll money in the till. Bowerman handed out the weapons the morning of the heist. He had a sawed-off shotgun and a pistol; the others had a couple of pistols each. Chernick pulled up outside of the bank's front entrance in a green Oldsmobile he had stolen a couple of days before and let the other men out. Scholl entered by the front door. Bowerman and Vito went in the side door.

Bowerman jumped up on the counter and announced, "This is a stickup! Get your hands up!" While Scholl told the customers and employees to move against the wall, Vito jumped over the counter and started stuffing money into a large bag. (It was later found that he had collected $140,769.) "Get down, everybody!" Bowerman shouted. Unknown to the robbers, bank teller Alice Ruzicka had hit the alarm. A telephone repairman in the back of the bank saw what was happening and called the police. Corporal Robert Heitz and Officer Melburn Stein were only two blocks away when the call came over their radio. They rushed to the bank, followed by dozens of police officers and newspaper photographers. The commotion drew a crowd outside.

The robbers saw the two policemen approaching the bank. One of them yelled, "The heat! The coppers!" Heitz went in the side door, while Stein rushed to the front door. They exchanged gunfire with the robbers. Heitz was hit in the head and neck by a blast from Bowerman's shotgun and in the shoulder by a round from Vito's pistol. (Heitz recovered from his wounds.) One of Heitz's shots hit Scholl in the back. "Grab a woman!" Bowerman

Police crouching behind cars outside Southwest Bank during the bank robbery. *Courtesy of the St. Louis Mercantile Library at the University of Missouri–St. Louis.*

yelled, and he seized a customer named Eva Hamilton. He started out the front door. Stein shot Bowerman in the chest as he emerged from the bank. Hamilton fell to the ground, fracturing both of her wrists.

Scholl crawled toward the back of the bank as bullets whizzed into the bank lobby from the police outside. Vito asked Scholl if he was hit, and he replied that he was. Vito said, "I can't take a pinch," and shot himself in the head. Just then, the police fired tear gas into the bank. Scholl tried to get one of the customers to take his pistols, fearing that he would be shot if the police came in and saw him with them. The customer figured the same thing and refused to take them. Finally, the police burst into the lobby and took Scholl into custody. Chernick, who was supposed to drive the getaway car, got away all right but without his comrades. He drove off as soon as Heitz and Stein showed up. He was captured later in Chicago and returned to St. Louis for trial.

Bowerman died three days later. He admitted to the South Bend robbery but refused to say what happened to the take from that job. Scholl was convicted and received a twenty-five-year sentence. Chernick's legal problems turned into a saga. Chernick was charged with multiple crimes, including bank robbery and assault. One of the problems was that he was never in the bank, so the state's theory was that he was "constructively present" because he conspired with the others. He was tried three times before the prosecutor secured a sentence he liked. Chernick was in and out of trouble for the rest of his life. He was convicted in Illinois for burglary and was even picked up in Clayton, Missouri, for stealing $2.15 from a parking meter. Chernick died in 2003.

Charles Guggenheim was a filmmaker who set up a production company in St. Louis in 1954. His first motion picture, *A City Decides*, was an Oscar-nominated short film—today, we would call it a docudrama—about the integration of St. Louis schools in the wake of the *Brown v. Board of Education* decision outlawing segregated schools.

In looking for a new subject, Guggenheim hit on the idea of doing a movie about the Southwest Bank robbery—but not a documentary. Rather, it would be a noirish film that explored the characters' motivations and not just a shoot 'em up heist film. Guggenheim hired five professional Broadway actors for the leads, including Steve McQueen, who had just completed his only star turn on the New York stage. McQueen was a struggling actor whose first leading movie role was that of a teenager (he was twenty-seven at the time) in *The Blob*, a low-budget science fiction horror movie.

Guggenheim gave the characters fictional names, and some of the action was altered to fit the movie. Most notably, the young football player based on Glenn Chernick, Steve McQueen's character, was not the getaway driver. McQueen enters the bank with the other gunmen, gets shot, tries to give away his pistols and is hauled away by the paddy wagon, with his view out the vehicle's barred back windows as the final scene.

The film was shot entirely on location in St. Louis in October and November 1957. The outside shots of the bank were filmed at the actual Southwest Bank (which is still standing, although under another name). The interior shots of the robbery were filmed in a vacant former bank building downtown. The movie gang gathered in Tower Grove Park to discuss the heist, just as Bowerman and his men had in 1953.

Many of the extras were present at the scene of the 1953 robbery. Officer Stein played himself and shot the Bowerman character in the climactic gun battle, just as he had four years before. Another fifty St. Louis police officers were recruited to appear, and reporters and photographers who had been present played themselves.

A movie still from *The St. Louis Bank Robbery*. The officer holding the revolver is Melburn Stein, who played himself and reenacted the shooting of Fred Bowerman as he emerged from the bank with a hostage. *Courtesy of the Missouri Historical Society.*

The movie was released in 1959. The posters accompanying the movie proclaim its title as *The Great St. Louis Bank Robbery*, and it is usually referred to by that name. However, its actual title is *The St. Louis Bank Robbery*. Although it is considered a minor noir classic today, the movie was popular in St. Louis and nowhere else when released.

Both Guggenheim and McQueen went on to bigger things. Guggenheim specialized in short documentaries, for which he received thirteen Academy Award nominations and five Oscars. McQueen, nicknamed the "King of Cool," became a television star and, later, an even bigger success on the screen in movies such as *The Thomas Crown Affair* and *Bullitt*. He died from cancer in 1980.

6.

THE SWOPE MURDER CASE

As he approached his eighty-second birthday, Thomas Swope had evolved into the classic cranky old man. Maybe he had been cranky all his life. He came to Kansas City in 1857. Swope realized the town was strategically placed to take advantage of the burgeoning westward expansion. He started buying land until he owned most of what became downtown. He was even bestowed with the honorific title of "Colonel."

Swope had two brothers and two sisters but no wife or children. In 1909, he lived in a few of the twenty-six rooms in his mansion in Independence, along with his brother Logan's widow, Maggie, and her seven children, Chrisman, Frances, Thomas, Lucy, Margaret, Stella and Sarah. His cousin and perhaps closest confidante, Moss Hunton, also lived with them.

Swope was one of those people who cared more for people as a whole than for individuals in particular. He was a philanthropist whose greatest gift to the people of Kansas City was a donation of 1,354 acres that became Swope Park. It is said that he disliked the presence of people so much that he declined to attend the park's dedication.

Swope devised the kind of will that makes lawyers salivate because it was calculated to make someone—maybe almost everyone—unhappy. He owned real property worth about $3,600,000 (in 1909 dollars) and cash or assets readily reduced to cash worth $1,400,000. Swope's will provided that each of Logan's seven children would receive an equal share of real estate, except for Frances, whose share was worth about half as much. They would share equally in the residuary $1.4 million, but if any of the seven

Right: Thomas Swope. He donated the land for Swope Park in Kansas City. His unusual will allegedly led to his death as part of a complex murder plot. *Courtesy of the Library of Congress.*

Below: The Swope mansion in Independence, Missouri, had twenty-six rooms and was the site of three alleged murders. It no longer stands. *Courtesy of the Library of Congress.*

beneficiaries died unmarried and childless, that person's share of the residuary estate (or whatever was then left over) would be divided among the survivors. All of the nieces and nephews were unmarried and childless except Frances and Thomas.

Everyone in the family knew the terms of their dear uncle's will, and they knew that as his birthday drew near, he intended to change the will so that the $1.4 million would not go to his nieces and nephews, but to charity. Thus, the framework was set for the mystery to come.

Frances Swope Hyde was the devoted wife of Bennett Clark Hyde. She stood by him through three trials before finally divorcing him. *Courtesy of the Missouri Valley Special Collections, Kansas City Public Library, Kansas City, Missouri.*

We don't know why Swope chose to slight his niece Frances, but it may have had something to do with her choice of spouse. Over the opposition of her mother, Frances ran away and married Bennett Clark Hyde, a medical doctor. Hyde knew his Bible, could quote Shakespeare and had a beautiful singing voice. He was also something of a cad. As the police surgeon, he brutally mistreated an African American woman who was suffering from a drug overdose. Later, he wooed and bilked a couple of divorcées. The police fired him, and the divorcées sued him (he settled the cases). But despite Hyde's inauspicious history and troubled relationship with his mother-in-law, the Colonel and the doctor eventually hit it off. They discussed the classics and other learned subjects. In fact, Swope liked Hyde so much, he bought the doctor and his wife a house in Kansas City.

On Friday, October 1, 1909, a chain of events began that tore this family apart for all the world to see. Cousin Moss fell ill that evening with apoplexy or, as we would call it today, a cerebral hemorrhage. Dr. Hyde and another family physician, Dr. George Twyman, were called. In those days, the usual treatment for apoplexy was bleeding, which was supposed to relieve arterial pressure. So, Hyde began to bleed Moss—over Dr. Twyman's mild protests—until he had drained nearly two quarts of blood from his body. Whether or not it relieved the arterial pressure, we don't know. However, we do know that Moss died on Friday night.

Colonel Swope's nurse was Pearl Kellar. Kellar was described by author Giles Fowler as a person known for her competence, conscientiousness and complete lack of human warmth. When she appeared in the Colonel's bedroom on Saturday morning to start his daily regimen of iron, quinine and strychnine, she announced curtly that Cousin Moss had died. This depressing news was followed by even worse events.

Hyde visited the Colonel and decided that he needed some digestive medicine after breakfast. He took a white capsule out of a pink pill box. At first, Swope refused to take it, but Hyde finally persuaded the old man to down it. Within twenty minutes, the Colonel had gone into convulsions. Hyde pronounced the Colonel, like his cousin, the victim of apoplexy.

After a few minutes, Swope managed to say, "Oh, my God, I wish I were dead. I wish I had not taken that medicine." (Hyde claimed the Colonel did *not* utter that last sentence—one of many points on which his account and Kellar's would conflict.) Hyde ordered injections of strychnine to stimulate Swope's pulse (Kellar said it was already very rapid). Kellar searched for the pink pill box to see what was in it but never found it. Colonel Swope's wish was fulfilled the next day. His body was scarcely cold when the family lawyer insisted the grieving relatives gather in the study that very evening for the reading of the will (a dramatic custom that is no longer observed except in movies and on television). It was the will that Colonel Swope intended to change the very next week.

The pall of the deaths hung over the Swope household for weeks. On the night of Sunday, November 21, Hyde and his wife had dinner at the mansion. Curiously, they brought their own water in bottles. (The Hydes would later dispute that they were there on November 21.) About a week later, both Margaret and Chrisman felt ill. One of their servants suffered from similar symptoms. Dr. Twyman examined them and determined that they had contracted typhoid. It wasn't immediately clear how three people in the household had come down with that disease—it wasn't going around Independence or Kansas City at the time—but the incubation period was known to be seven days. Thus, whatever exposure that led to the disease had happened around November 21. Within a week, there were two more cases of typhoid identified among the residents of this one house in the area. The family hired a crew of five nurses to care for the sick.

Chrisman, who was a bit sickly to begin with, had the most serious case. On the morning of December 5, Hyde visited Chrisman. The doctor decided Chrisman needed something for his digestion and gave him what was described as a "capsule." (Hyde later denied having administered any such capsule.) Within twenty minutes, Chrisman began experiencing severe convulsions. The nurse called Hyde back into the room. After examining the patient, Hyde declared that he was suffering from meningitis, a known complication of typhoid fever.

The family called in Dr. Twyman and his son Elmer, who was also a physician, for a consultation. They found Chrisman in tetanic state, his body stiff as if he had tetanus, his eyes open and staring upward to the right and his skin with a bluish tint. Neither Dr. Twyman nor his son thought he was suffering from meningitis. Later, Dr. Twyman would say, "I did not gainsay that diagnosis, although I thought the picture of meningitis was not complete to my mind and so expressed myself to my son afterward." Dr. Elmer Twyman translated: "Well, he did not have meningitis."

Chrisman's condition waxed and waned over the next few hours. That night, Hyde once again had the nurse give Chrisman one of the mysterious capsules. (And once again, Hyde vehemently denied having done so.) As the evening became night, Chrisman's condition worsened. He experienced another round of convulsions and died at 9:50 p.m. on December 6, unmarried and childless. Frances's inheritance increased.

Lucy was traveling in Europe when these events transpired. Her mother called her home to be with the family. Maggie wanted Frances to meet Lucy in New York to escort her home, but Hyde finagled things so that he got the job. While Hyde was on his trip east, the health of everyone in the mansion improved. Hyde met Lucy at the docks. That evening, they boarded the train for the trip to Kansas City. Lucy was thirsty and started to get a drink from the cooler down the aisle. Hyde volunteered to fetch it. He was gone for what seemed like a long time but finally returned. Lucy downed the water without a second thought. The next day, as they boarded the train from St. Louis to Kansas City, Lucy felt ill. When she arrived home, her mother insisted that she stay with friends instead of going to the family mansion on the stern advice of nurse Kellar. But a week after her sip of water on the train, Lucy came down with typhoid.

On December 18, Hyde came to the house to examine Margaret. He noticed a box of pills in her room that had been prescribed by Dr. Twyman. He examined them and directed the nurse to give one of them to Margaret after her bath. Within twenty minutes of taking the pill out of the box Hyde had handled, Margaret experienced the same kind of convulsions the Colonel and Chrisman had. Fortunately, Dr. Twyman appeared and gave her medication that eased the condition. Dr. Twyman shook his head and exclaimed, "I cannot see any cause for this convulsion." Nurse Kellar replied, "Dr. Twyman, have you ever noticed this is the third one in this house to have convulsions lately?" When Dr. Twyman came downstairs from

Margaret's bedroom, the nurses confronted him. Nurse Kellar, their leader, demanded that Hyde not be allowed to treat the patients anymore. "If he goes, we will stay. If he stays, we will go."

Twyman was in a quandary. Was Hyde a bad—or perhaps unlucky—physician, or was he something much worse? He consulted the Swope family lawyer, John Paxton, who lived nearby. They agreed that Twyman should return to the Swope home that night to lay what facts he knew before Maggie, and recommend that Hyde not be allowed there. Dr. Twyman duly trudged back to the house in the snow. Maggie had her suspicions, but when Twyman told her that the nurses refused to work with Hyde and why, she had a "great revelation," and things "appeared in a different light." She asked Twyman to deliver the news. Twyman asked her to tell Hyde to call him at the office when he came in.

In the meantime, Maggie talked things over with her son Thomas, who, with sister Lucy, was visiting that night. Thomas left to escort Lucy back to her temporary quarters. Hyde showed up, talked to Twyman on the telephone and agreed to see him that night. Thomas was returning from escorting his sister when he saw a figure walking up the opposite side of the street. The person stopped, took something out of his overcoat, dropped it on the ground and stomped on it. As the man passed under a streetlight, Thomas could see that he was Hyde. Thomas crossed over to the spot where the item lay. He saw it was a crushed capsule. Thomas hurriedly scooped up the remains and took them back to the mansion. He, his mother and one of the nurses said the capsule gave off an odd smell—the smell of bitter almonds that is characteristic of cyanide. (Hyde, needless to say, denied that he dropped or crushed anything on his walk to Twyman's office.)

When Hyde arrived at Dr. Twyman's office, the latter gave him the bad news that Maggie did not want him to come to the house anymore. Twyman said that the nurses refused to work with him and would leave if he was allowed back. "Well, that is pretty bad, isn't it?" Hyde said. When Hyde asked why the nurses refused to work with him, Twyman told him that the nurses believed he had killed Colonel Swope and Chrisman Swope by giving them some sort of poisonous capsule and that he had caused the household to be infected with typhoid, apparently in the hope that the deaths of some or all of Frances's siblings would bring her more money. Hyde, remarkably calm, said, "Well, that looks pretty bad, that is a terrible accusation. I could sue those nurses for a criminal accusation like that."

After Hyde left to recover his things from the mansion, Dr. Twyman called lawyer Paxton and recounted his interview. Paxton rushed to meet Maggie to decide what to do next. She was in what Giles Fowler calls a prosecutorial mood. It was a mood in which she would remain for years.

Over the next few days, Paxton initiated an investigation that turned up a number of disturbing facts. In September, Hyde had purchased four capsules of potassium cyanide, ostensibly to use against some dogs that were plaguing his office, although it seemed strange to the pharmacist that he would use capsules and not powder for that purpose. The substance was ordinarily used by dentists and jewelers as a solvent in working with gold. He bought a dozen more capsules in early December; these, Hyde later testified, were to be used to kill roaches.

In November, Hyde had taken an interest in setting up his own laboratory. A local bacteriologist, Dr. Edward Stewart, agreed to provide him with some cultures, including one of typhoid. After the outbreak of typhoid at the Swope mansion, Stewart sneaked into Hyde's laboratory and found that enough of the typhoid culture was gone to infect "the whole of Kansas City."

With the family's suspicions heightened, Paxton and Thomas Swope traveled to Chicago to engage the services of Doctors Luther Hektoen, a pathologist; Walter Haines, a toxicologist; and Victor Vaughn, a chemist. Haines and Vaughn found cyanide in the crushed capsule that had been retrieved by Thomas Swope and traces of strychnine in a bottle of Margaret's vomit that had been obtained after she was treated by Hyde.

Dr. Hektoen came to Kansas City to perform autopsies on the bodies of Chrisman and the Colonel. He found no evidence that Chrisman had died from meningitis as Hyde had claimed. There was evidence, however, that Chrisman had suffered from typhoid, but Hektoen determined that it had not been severe enough to have been the cause of his death. The autopsy did find traces of strychnine in Chrisman's liver. The Colonel's body had lain in a vault in the cemetery's mausoleum for three months, where it had become frozen. Dr. Hektoen proceeded to examine the Colonel's brain and other organs. He found no evidence of apoplexy—Hyde's diagnosis. A later analysis of the Colonel's liver tissues showed it contained one-sixth of a grain of strychnine, which, when extrapolated to the entire body, was a lethal dose. A coroner's jury was convened to determine the cause of the Colonel's death. Nurse Kellar recounted how Hyde had given a capsule from the mysterious pill box to the Colonel, who then went promptly into convulsions, leading to his demise. The coroner asked her, "Do you know anything that might have caused Colonel Swope's death other than that capsule?" She replied, "I do not." Dr. Hektoen rendered his opinion that the Colonel was poisoned.

Maggie Swope testified about the Colonel's will and said that everyone in the family knew about it and that he intended to change it. Although Hyde promised before the hearing to give his side under oath, when the much-anticipated time came for him to take the stand, he declined. The coroner's jury returned a finding that Colonel Swope had died from strychnine poisoning from the capsule Hyde had given him. However, they said, "Whether with felonious intent, we, the jury, are unable to decide."

The Swope family picked up the cost of the prosecution, including the hiring of a special prosecutor. The man selected was James Reed, an associate of the Pendergast machine who was elected as a United States senator later that year. He was a formidable trial advocate. One Kansas City paper described him as a tall, graceful man whose appearance suggested "an ivory and gray steel scabbard, sheathing a rapier of white hot attack." His opponent was defense counsel Frank Walsh, a stocky, bull-headed man who earned his reputation while representing labor unions. These legal titans had clashed before. In 1899, Walsh had represented Jesse Edward James, the son of the famous outlaw who was accused of train robbery just as the elder Jesse had been. The prosecutor was James Reed. Grandmother Zerelda provided young Jesse with an alibi, just as she had done for his father years before, but in this case, a number of other reliable witnesses corroborated her testimony. Jesse was acquitted, reputedly one of the only two cases Reed ever lost. Jesse turned to the practice of law, working with Walsh to represent railroad workers in cases against their employers.

After three weeks of testimony, a grand jury handed down eleven indictments against Hyde, charging him with the first-degree murders of Colonel Swope and Chrisman Swope, the negligent killing of Cousin Moss Hunton by excessive bleeding and attempts to kill Margaret and other members of the household by infecting them with typhoid.

The prosecution decided to try Hyde first for the death of Colonel Swope. The trial was set for April 11, 1910. Reed rose to tell the jury what the prosecution was going to prove. He said that he would show that Hyde devised a plan that only a physician could carry out, that he intended "to exterminate the entire Swope family" and that he did it to gain "great wealth." Reed started to detail all of the accusations against Hyde, but Walsh leaped to his feet to interrupt him. Walsh vehemently objected to any evidence concerning what had happened to Chrisman or the other members of the Swope family being admitted because Hyde was only on trial for the Colonel's death. Walsh's objection was based on the well-known legal principle that the jury should not hear about other alleged criminal acts the defendant may have committed because they may convict him of being an all-around bad person instead of finding him guilty beyond a reasonable doubt of committing the crime for which he was charged. The judge, however, overruled Walsh based on the exception that, when evidence of other crimes was so intertwined with the crime charged, it is admissible to show a common scheme. It was a risky tactic on the prosecution's part, but it allowed Reed and his fellow prosecutors to wallow in the details of the others' deaths and illnesses.

Nurse Kellar was the first witness, and she was an impressive one. She recounted the convulsions, the deaths, the diseases, the capsules and her suspicions. Walsh went after Kellar with all of his legal artillery, but she could not be budged from her story. A Kansas City newspaper reported that she was "easily one of the best, coolest, most resourceful witnesses.... Nothing ruffles her, no attack destroys her poise or takes away from the cool, watchful calculation of her black eyes."

Witness after witness marched to the stand, describing the disasters that afflicted the Swope mansion. The state wrapped up its case with a parade of experts the prosecutors no doubt believed would put the final touches on their theory of Hyde's nefarious scheme.

Dr. Frank Hall, a pathologist, testified that the Colonel died of poisoning. Under a brutal cross-examination by Walsh, Hall conceded that the old gentleman's kidneys were atrophied and that he could have died of uremic poisoning. Dr. Hektoen came next and fared no better. Dr. Hektoen gave his opinions that Chrisman did not have meningitis and that the Colonel's autopsy showed he was poisoned and didn't die as a result of apoplexy. On cross-examination, Walsh went to work. *Didn't tissues from Chrisman's show signs of meningitis?* Well, yes. *Didn't you write in the leading textbook on autopsies that removing organs from a frozen body would compromise the accuracy of the results?* Well, yes, Hektoen conceded, to the delight of the audience. Drs. Haines and Vaughn stuck to their guns about finding poison, but the damage was done. The prosecution topped off their case by calling Maggie Swope to the stand, where she tearfully spoke of her last visit with Chrisman. She told him on his death bed, "I won't let anyone hurt you, Chrisman, or deceive you." The state rested.

The defense opened its case by calling the first of nine experts to challenge everything the prosecution's doctors had said. The dullness of the scientific testimony was finally relieved when Walsh brought his own tear-jerking witness to the stand—Frances Hyde. Frances was in what the newspapers of the day called "a delicate condition." In other words, she was pregnant. She

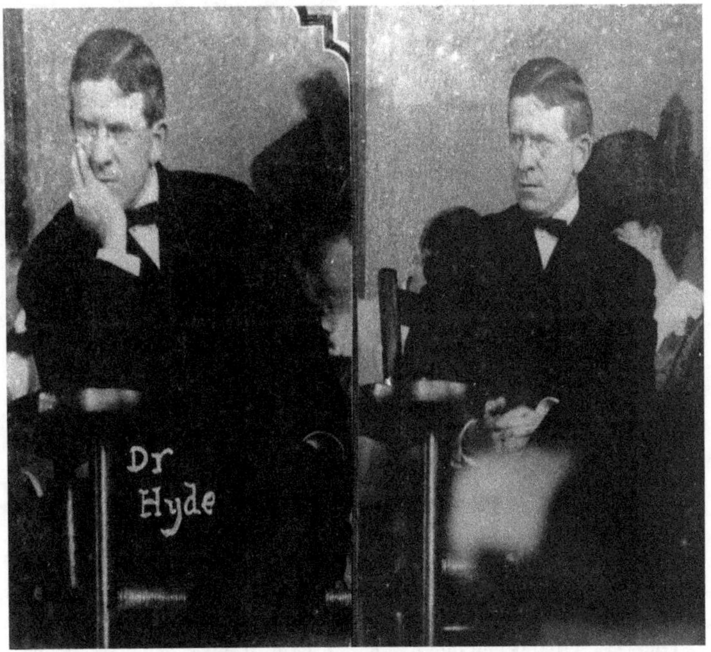

Dr. Bennett Clark Hyde, MD, testifying at his trial. *Courtesy of the Missouri Valley Special Collections, Kansas City Public Library, Kansas City, Missouri.*

contradicted every claim made by the family and the nurses. In particular, she said that Thomas never discovered any capsule the night of December 18 because she was with him the entire time until Maggie asked her and her husband to leave. This left only one more person to support the defense—Bennett Clark Hyde himself.

Hyde, of course, denied everything. Either the incriminating actions did not occur or they were completely innocent when taken in context. He braced himself for the expected storm of cross-examination by the formidable James Reed. But instead, the Jackson County prosecutor, Virgil Conkling, who had been shunted aside by the Swope family, was chosen to deliver the blows.

For five hours, Conkling went after Hyde, who was, as the *Kansas City Post* described him, at times "nervous, at times, irritable, and plainly belligerent." The prosecutor highlighted Hyde's purchase of cyanide capsules (even though no one testified that Colonel Swope, almost the forgotten victim, had cyanide in his body). Hyde evaded the questions, gave preposterous answers and couldn't explain to anyone's satisfaction what they were for. It was, as the *Kansas City Times* said, "as merciless an inquisition as one is likely to hear in a courtroom."

The closing arguments were as spectacular as everyone expected from such towering legal talent. Reed, in particular, delivered one of his best speeches, declaring that "the typhoid followed that man like sharks follow a ship laden with dead." The jury retired on Friday night to deliberate. Saturday passed with no news. Likewise, there was no verdict on Sunday. At 10:15 a.m. on Monday, May 16, 1910, the jury came back with a guilty verdict. Hyde was taken to jail to await the results of his appeal.

No time in jail is easy, but it cannot be said that Hyde had to endure the kind of hard time that one usually associates with a convicted murderer. Frances brought him home-cooked meals, and he was allowed whatever reading material he desired. The authorities promised he would be released long enough to be by his wife's side when she delivered their baby, but they reneged. Sadly, the baby did not survive long. The only good news Hyde received was that the Missouri Supreme Court reversed his conviction. The risk Reed took in introducing evidence of other alleged crimes was found to be cause for a new trial because those events—the death of Cousin Moss Hunton and the typhoid outbreak—were too tenuous a link to justify bringing them before the jury.

The second trial began on October 23, 1911. It proceeded at a plodding, but presumably error-free, pace when it was interrupted by a bizarre incident a month and a half after it began. Juryman Harry Waldron became so homesick for his wife that he squeezed over the transom in the hotel where the jury was sequestered and fled. He was gone for two days before he turned himself in. The judge found Waldron to be mentally unsound and declared a mistrial. The Swope family soldiered on, financing a third prosecution of Hyde. This time, the jury could not reach a unanimous decision—the vote was 9–3 for not guilty—and another mistrial was declared. After spending $250,000 on the prosecutions of Bennett Clark Hyde, Maggie Swope finally gave up. There was no fourth trial. Hyde was free.

Although she couldn't convict Hyde, Maggie did manage to ruin his life. The Jackson County Medical Society, which elected him president before the deaths began, kicked him out after his conviction. Frances divorced him in 1920. Hyde went home to Lexington, Missouri, where he lived a quiet life, practicing medicine until his death in 1934. Maggie herself went broke. But Thomas Swope's legacy and the beautiful park named after him remain.

7.

THE PROSECUTOR'S WIFE

Around 11:30 p.m. on the evening of July 14, 1916, Oscar McDaniel, the prosecuting attorney of Buchanan County, Missouri, received a phone call from a nearby saloon, informing him that his brother was there and drinking too much and that he should come pick him up. Oscar immediately drove to the saloon. The call was a hoax. This raised a warning flag in Oscar's mind, and he rushed back to his home, where his wife and two of their three children were asleep in their beds. (The third child was spending time with his grandparents.)

He parked his car in front of the garage, and shots were fired at him from behind a tree south of the garage entrance. Oscar returned fire, aiming in the direction he saw the shots coming from. Both shooters missed their marks. At that point, the "assassin," as the *St. Joseph Gazette* called the shooter, fled. Oscar hurried inside, worried about his family.

On entering his bedroom, Oscar found his wife, Harriet, lying on the floor, brutally beaten around the head. He spoke to her, but she did not answer. Oscar checked on the children, who were unharmed; he lifted his wife to the bed and washed the blood from her face. He then called for police and medical help. Harriet was rushed to Ensworth Hospital, where she was not expected to pull through. She died early the next morning without regaining consciousness. Apparently, the assassin did not awaken or enter the room where two of the McDaniel children were sleeping.

All of the members of the police force were called in to work on the case immediately. Search dogs were also quickly brought to the scene, and

Sarah Harriet Moss McDaniel's murder is still unsolved. *Courtesy of the* St. Joseph News-Press.

they followed a trail throughout the neighborhood. The bloodhounds led searchers to a rooming house, where they were taken inside to check the rooms and hallways. Several men from the boardinghouse were arrested, and others were placed under surveillance after the owner reported seeing a suspicious man in the rooms during the night.

The police theorized the assassin had entered and exited the house through a rear basement window. He (and there was no discussion that the assailant was anything but a man) attacked Harriet while she slept, giving her no chance to defend herself. The bedroom drawers were ransacked, and Harriet's gold band, diamond ring worth about $300 and a small amount of cash were taken. The police believed that the condition of the room and the taking of the rings and money was simply to make the intrusion look like a burglary.

The first suspects who were considered were James Carboy, someone from his gang, and a member of the Industrial Workers of the World

(IWW). The IWW members had been involved in incidents recently, and James Carboy was an escapee from a mental hospital who had been committed after he pleaded insanity at a recent trial for robbery. Threatening letters that had been sent to Prosecutor McDaniel were also investigated. Eleven men were held the next day for further investigation; all of them were members of gangs Oscar had recently prosecuted. Oscar had received a letter that threatened his family would be "blown to hell" unless he released a certain prisoner. After receiving that threat, he had started carrying a revolver.

Another theory was that the murder of Harriet and attempted assassination of Oscar were parts of a bigger plot to engineer a jail break and attack the county prison with dynamite. The gang responsible for the suspected plot was considered very dangerous. At the center of the gang was James Barrett, who had been in prison for five years on a holdup charge and was soon to be tried on other charges. It was believed Barrett was the author of the letter threatening harm to the McDaniel family. The entire investigation was carried out under strict secrecy, with no information given to the press. After the death of Harriet McDaniel, feelings ran at a fever pitch among the citizenry, and a threat of lynching the suspect was often voiced. Special precautions were taken at the jail to guard against mob action. However, none of these theories was ever proven.

A coroner's inquest was called and a special prosecutor, Bart Lockwood, appointed. The first hint that there was a suspicion surrounding Oscar McDaniel occurred when Harriet's mother was questioned about the state of the McDaniels' marriage. She said she knew of no discord. This interest was later explained as an effort to clear up the many rumors that there were problems between Oscar and Harriet.

Oscar McDaniel testified to his movements on the evening before the murder. He had visited his lodge for a short time and then made his way to several locations to investigate various complaints his office had received. He was preparing for bed when he received the phone call that led to him leaving his wife and family alone in the house.

There was some questioning regarding the handling of the investigation by the police. Within an hour of the discovery of the murder, many people who had no police business were wandering through the house—some only to take in the gory details. C.A. Cook and another party burned the sheets and mattress from the bed and cleaned the room, Cook testified, with permission from the police "because people were coming." Police officials who were questioned on the stand admitted there was no active theory in the case and said they did not know who murdered Harriet McDaniel. Yet, there was plenty of gossip about the case.

At the inquest, a good part of the questioning was aimed at either refuting or substantiating the rumors and gossip surrounding the murder of Harriet McDaniel. One aspect of the gossip concerned the McDaniels' marriage. Mr. and Mrs. Orestes Mitchell were questioned and identified as friends of the McDaniels. Mr. Mitchell was an attorney for Dagmar Krucker, who was granted a divorce on the day Harriet was murdered. Oscar represented John Krucker. Both the Mitchells said the McDaniels enjoyed a happy marriage. Krucker, in his testimony, said that both he and his wife were friends of the McDaniels and that he sometimes picked up his daughter at their home after his separation from his wife. Mrs. Krucker also said that she was friends with both Harriet and Oscar and had been for many years. She said she had gone downtown with Harriet the Wednesday before the murder. Mrs. Krucker was asked if she had ever met with Oscar in Kansas City, and she said she had not. The hint, although never overtly expressed, was that perhaps Oscar's interest in Dagmar had something to do with the murder. Neighbors of the McDaniel family testified that they heard screams on the night of the murder between 10:00 p.m. and 10:45 p.m., and then they heard no other unusual sounds until the shots.

A month later, the inquest was still active, the murder was still being investigated and there was nothing viable to go on. Some things that were in great supply were threatening letters with various confessions to the murder, but none of them withstood investigation. Bart Lockwood, the special prosecutor who was handling the matter, employed a private detective to look into the case, but the court refused to pay the bill, bringing that investigation to a halt.

During the entire process of the coroner's inquest and investigation, Oscar McDaniel was running his campaign for re-election as prosecuting attorney.

The coroner's investigation ended on September 6, 1916, with the following verdict:

> *We, the jury, find that Harriet McDaniel came to her death as the result of being struck feloniously on the head with a deadly weapon, the exact nature of which is unknown, by a person or persons unknown to the jurors, and we recommend that a vigorous investigation be continued by the proper authorities: We furthermore respectfully demand that a special grand jury be called to thoroughly investigate to the end that the guilty party or parties be brought to justice.*

Oscar agreed with the coroner's jury that a grand jury should be called as soon as possible. He said that testimony could be offered under the secrecy of the grand jury proceeding that perhaps could not be given in a public setting. The judge decreed that no grand jury would be called. This left the case in the hands of Lockwood and the prosecutor's office.

When the court decided it was illegal to pay for a private investigator, Bart Lockwood and the *St. Joseph News-Press* started a campaign to raise private funds. Oscar McDaniel made the offer to pay the legitimate costs involved in an investigation himself, but his offer was turned down.

On September 24, 1916, Oscar McDaniel was arrested for the murder of his wife, Harriet Moss McDaniel. His response when police detectives showed up with the warrant was a simple: "All right." He asked to walk to the station rather than have the police wagon called, and the detectives granted his request. They stopped along the way so Oscar could buy cigars. Special Prosecutor Bart Lockwood accused McDaniel of interfering with the investigation and intimidating witnesses. He said he would not recommend bail. He also requested again that a grand jury be called.

Oscar talked freely to reporters, saying that all he wanted was an early trial. He was running for prosecutor, and he didn't want the questions of his guilt or innocence to get in the way of his election. He also said he did not have any intention of withdrawing. He issued the following statement:

> *The statements of Mr. Lockwood and his Burns "framer," calculated to prejudge me as guilty in the public mind before I have had an opportunity to have a trial is absolutely false. In a spirit of fairness to me, I ask the public to withhold judgment until all the facts are known. Mother Grundies have circulated countless false and slanderous rumors about me, and some have tried to blacken the fair name of my wife after she is gone.*
>
> *It seemed not enough in their sight that my wife, whom I have known and loved since she was a twelve-year-old girl, should be torn from me. They hope to assassinate the character and destroy the future of the only one left to care for and safeguard the welfare of my three motherless children.*

The paper also published a copy of Oscar's record of convictions while he was prosecutor and his request for an early trial. He asked the police commissioner to assign two or three officers to investigate his wife's murder. Later, Oscar stated that his arrest was a plot to defeat him in the election for prosecuting attorney. When asked by a reporter from the *Topeka* (Kansas) *Daily Capital* if he denied killing his wife, Oscar replied, "Why, hell, yes I do."

Sarah Harriet Moss McDaniel poses with her three children. *Courtesy of the* St. Joseph News-Press.

Oscar was transferred to the hospital ward of the county jail. He was to remain incarcerated until the grand jury inquiry ended. He was the only inmate there and had more freedom than he would have had in the general population. For example, Oscar viewed an air show and ate lunch at a local café in the company of one of the deputies. He also visited his children at home. Lockwood and the sheriff received letters threatening to blow up the jail and the courthouse if the amount of freedom given to Oscar during his jail time was not curtailed. The sheriff said Oscar was treated as a "trusty" at the jail and that his freedoms were not unusual. The letter was dismissed as one of many threats.

The three McDaniel children (Helen, age eight; Marion, age six; and Odell, age fourteen) experienced their own difficult times during their father's incarceration. They attended the Hall School and reported that their classmates treated them unkindly "because their daddy is in jail." They came home in tears nightly, telling their grandmother that other children ran from them or asked that their seats be moved away from them. The principal announced that any child who treated the McDaniel children badly would be sent home until they apologized, and he said their name would be published in the paper.

The grand jury continued to look into the McDaniels' marital relationship and Oscar's exact locations from the time he left his lodge until he returned home. Following this line of inquiry, one of the witnesses was expected to testify about an argument between Harriet and Oscar about a mutual family friend. The friend had told the witness of this argument, and she phoned the witness after the murder, asking her not to speak about it. Neighbors who had heard a scream coming from the McDaniel home between 10:00 p.m. and 10:30 p.m. were also called. One witness testified to the scream and added that angry words and raised voices preceded that scream. This testimony was not corroborated. The timing of the screams that were heard by neighbors was important to figuring out what Oscar did between leaving the lodge and arriving home at 11:15 p.m. Did he arrive home earlier? Telephone operators also appeared and said no phone calls had been received at the McDaniels' home between 10:00 p.m. and 12:15 a.m., disputing the claim that Oscar had received a call during that time period to come pick up his brother at a local saloon. A manager said it wasn't possible for the operators to know if a particular number received a call or not. The question of the weapon continued to be discussed, as the exact weapon that was used was never agreed on, nor was one found, despite numerous attempts to locate it.

Oscar's campaign to be re-elected as prosecuting attorney of Buchanan County also continued throughout the trial. Lockwood, the special prosecutor, charged that the men holding political rallies for Oscar were, in reality, trying the case at those rallies. Some party officials felt that the case was hurting other Democratic candidates and tried to keep Oscar's representatives from speaking at their gatherings. Oscar refused to withdraw his name from the ballot.

Finally, on October 10, 1916, an indictment was issued against Oscar McDaniel for the murder of his wife. Oscar waived a formal arraignment and entered a not guilty plea. He appeared unconcerned and stated that he was not at all surprised at the grand jury outcome. A trial date was set for October 18. Oscar was released on $50,000 bail the next day, although the special prosecutor submitted that capital cases (hinting at a possible request for the death penalty) were not bailable. The judge also ruled that Oscar could continue serving as the prosecuting attorney. He immediately stepped out to campaign for re-election as prosecuting attorney that evening with a speech asking his supporters, who listened respectfully, to withhold judgment until the trial was over and he was found not guilty.

The jury pool was expanded from its usual number to 125 people because of the high visibility of the case. The court believed it would be difficult to find jurors who had not already formed an opinion regarding Oscar's guilt or innocence. Attorney General John Barker, who was brought in to help with the trial, found it surprising that so many jurors claimed they had not already decided whether or not Oscar was guilty. It became more and more evident with the questioning of the potential jurors that the prosecution was set on asking for the death penalty. Even Oscar himself appeared unsettled as he chewed on a half-smoked cigar during the course of questioning. Suddenly, the trial was delayed to investigate the manner in which the jury was drawn. This left Oscar in the position of having to face voters before he faced a jury.

At the same time, across the state, in St. Louis, Missouri, a man named McDaniel was also running for circuit attorney, the equivalent of the prosecuting attorney in Buchanan County. This McDaniel received letters threatening the "same dose Mrs. Oscar D. McDaniel got in St. Joseph" against his wife. Mrs. McDaniel grew so upset by these letters that the family was moved out of town to a safe place until the election was over.

Once the jury selection was called into question, the campaign took front and center. On the Sunday before the election, the *St. Joseph Gazette* published an interview with Harriet's family members (mother and siblings) who claimed she was unhappy. One family member was quoted as saying, "How about the other women? When Oscar is mentioning his love for Harriet, why doesn't he say something of the other woman in the case?" The reporter continued by observing that the household seemed convinced of another woman in the case. When attacked by Oscar's campaign, they told a reporter they stood by their statements in the interview. The campaign countered with an advertisement in the competing *St. Joseph News-Press* detailing Harriet's mother's sworn testimony that her daughter was happy in her marriage, that her husband treated her well and that she had no knowledge of any infidelity on Oscar's part. Despite every attempt, Oscar D. McDaniel lost his race for re-election as prosecuting attorney of Buchanan County.

On the Thursday following the election, a new jury pool was drawn, and jury selection was, for the second time, ready to begin. The potential jurors were quickly examined and installed.

The main question of the trial was the time at which Harriet McDaniel was killed. The prosecution's case and its supporting witnesses contended that she was killed between 10:30 p.m. and 10:45 p.m. The defense stuck with the original story that it occurred sometime after Oscar McDaniel left at 11:15 p.m. One of the biggest problems for the prosecution was that its case was entirely circumstantial. The defense's problem was that it could not peg any suspect as the "burglar" it asserted murdered Harriet. Lockwood also planned to show that Oscar had grown tired of Harriet and had become enamored of another woman. He chose to kill her to avoid any action, such as separation or divorce, that would affect his career.

The police surgeon, the first doctor to see Harriet McDaniel after the attack, dealt two blows to Oscar during his testimony. He said that Harriet was struck while sitting, not lying in the bed, and he said that she never laid in the pool of blood on the floor as Oscar said she had been when he found her. He also surmised that she was struck with a left-handed blow from someone standing in front of and above her. Oscar was left-handed.

The state met a roadblock when the testimony of a private detective was restricted. Harriet was said to have consulted the detective to collect evidence against her husband to use in a divorce proceeding. If this testimony was disallowed or if Oscar had no knowledge of it, there would be no evidence of motive. The detective was allowed to testify that Harriet had consulted him in regard to having her husband watched but was not permitted to recount any conversations between himself and the victim. The last witness before the prosecution rested its case was Harriet's sister Allene Moss, who also was not allowed to testify to any conversations the two had regarding the state of the McDaniel marriage.

When the state rested, it had only called thirty-one of the one hundred witnesses it had listed, with all but two witnesses being the same as those who were heard at the grand jury. Most disappointing to the viewers in the courtroom was the failure to call Mrs. Dagmar Krucker, who was frequently mentioned in reference to the possible discord in the McDaniel marriage.

Much of the prosecution's case was based on the McDaniels' neighbors having heard a scream the night of the murder. The defense presented a witness who said she was visiting in that neighborhood the same night and had screamed when she was frightened by being pushed too high in a swing. The defense attorney also dramatically accused a private detective engaged by Bart Lockwood of conspiring with the special prosecutor against Oscar. The defense also called John Krucker regarding the relationship between his divorce from his wife, Dagmar, and the murder. He denied any connection at all between his marital affairs and the McDaniels' marriage.

Oscar McDaniel took the witness stand in his own defense on the Wednesday before Thanksgiving. He was dressed in a black suit, black tie, white shirt and black shoes. His voice was firm and could be heard throughout the courtroom. He did not hesitate when answering the questions put to him. By the end of his story regarding the evening of the murder and his movements that night, the general opinion throughout the courtroom was that he had favorably impressed the jury. His testimony also touched on the rivalry between Oscar and the special prosecutor, Bart Lockwood. At one time, they had both been candidates for prosecuting attorney. Oscar dropped out of that election and threw his support behind a third candidate, not Lockwood. The McDaniels' oldest child, Odell, was the final witness to testify. Attorneys asked whether his mother and father were happy together, and he answered that they were. At the conclusion of Odell's testimony, the defense rested its case. Court was adjourned until after Thanksgiving. Jurors continued to be sequestered and had to celebrate the holiday away from their families.

After a parade of rebuttal witnesses and closing arguments, the case was submitted to the jury on Tuesday, December 5. Oscar McDaniel was found not guilty of the murder of his wife, Sarah Harriet Moss McDaniel. The jury deliberated for less than two hours.

The case continued to appear in the news and in the gossip, no doubt, of St. Joseph. Dagmar Krucker was murdered by her ex-husband, John, on Sunday, February 18, 1917. After shooting Dagmar in the heart, John tried to commit suicide but survived the bullet to his head. Two motives were advanced. John had tried to convince Dagmar to marry him again, and she had originally agreed, then backed out. The second was that he had heard a rumor that she had married Oscar McDaniel. Krucker was charged with murder while he was still in the hospital recovering from his self-inflicted head wound. He died as a result of that wound in May 1917, before he could be tried.

Barely a year after the murder of Harriet, Oscar married Zora Cook in a private ceremony at his home. He continued to practice law across the hall from Bart Lockwood, the man who had prosecuted him. In February 1919, the family home where Harriet had been murdered was burned nearly to the ground. Oscar saved his wife and children by lowering them to safety from the second floor using a rope. Later that year, in April, a notice appeared on the door of his law office, stating, "Persons having business with Oscar D. McDaniel are referred to Sherman & Otis." McDaniel moved his family to a farm in southern Kansas and left no forwarding address.

Oscar D. McDaniel died in June 1936 in Washington, D.C., where he had lived for less than a year. At that time, he was no longer going by

Oscar. He had his name legally changed to Russell McDrew. For years, Oscar had lived in California, where his two surviving children, Helen and Marion, still lived. His second wife, Zora, died in California, and he married a third time. His body was secretly returned to St. Joseph for burial under his new name beside Harriet in Mt. Mora Cemetery. There were no mourners and no service at the grave of Russell McDrew, and flowers were arranged to hide the engraving on the tombstone over his burial spot so as not to give away the secret. One secret, however, still remains—who killed Harriet McDaniel?

8.

ANGEL OF MERCY OR ANGEL OF DEATH?

Bertha Williams, a farm girl, was born October 30, 1871, in Morse Mill, Jefferson County, Missouri. She was considered a beauty as a young woman, petite with auburn hair and blue eyes. In 1894, she married Henry Graham and ran a hotel with her husband in the area where she was born and grew up. Two years later, their one child, a daughter named Lila, was born. For most women of the time, this would have been their entire story, but Bertha's diverged when she and Henry started having marital problems in 1905. It was rumored that Henry was seeing other women, so when Gene Gifford, a man ten years her junior, moved to town, Bertha was attracted to him, and the two began an affair. Still, Bertha and Henry remained married until he died of pneumonia while under Bertha's care in 1906. Bertha collected on Henry's life insurance policy and used that money to start her new life as Mrs. Eugene Gifford in Catawissa, Franklin County, Missouri, in 1907.

Gene was well-liked in the community and was considered a hard worker, but there were mixed opinions where Bertha was concerned. Business visitors to the home found Bertha rather cold and not very communicative, but it was said she was an excellent cook. And that is how she became known in the surrounding area. She was a good cook and a nurse, and she was willing to help whenever anyone was ill. Medical help was scarce in the area, with only one doctor available, so Bertha's ministrations were welcome. Like many others, she concocted her own medicines.

Bertha's mother-in-law, Emily Gifford, moved in with the couple in 1912; she was fifty-four at the time (considered old in the early twentieth century). She died soon after joining the family of "aortic regurgitation," according to the examining doctor. Since she was old, her death was not considered out of the ordinary.

Gene's twelve-year-old brother joined the family with his mother. He died in May 1913 of "strangulation due to an accumulation of mucus and an inability to expectorate," believed to be a complication of whooping cough. There were no antibiotics or vaccines to treat or prevent this illness. Bertha and Gene named their son, who was born in 1914, James after Gene's brother.

In February 1915, a neighbor's son, fifteen-month-old Bennett Stuhlfelder, developed pneumonia. As she often did, Bertha volunteered to take care of him. She spent three days and nights with him as he suffered from severe stomach pain. He died on February 26. The diagnosis was bronchopneumonia.

Gene brought his cousin Sherman Pounds, a forty-nine-year-old widower, home in February 1917. Pounds was drunk. Bertha treated him with one of her homemade tonics, and he died after suffering from severe stomach cramps. The doctor attributed his death to acute alcoholism.

In November 1917, Bertha traveled to nearby Pacific, Missouri, to purchase, she claimed, arsenic to be used as rat poison. When purchasing arsenic, buyers had to sign a register, and this record of her acquisition would prove very important later in her life.

Only two days later, one of the hired hands on the Gifford farm, James Lewis Ogle, grew ill, and the doctor diagnosed him with malaria. As he continued to deteriorate, even with Bertha's care, he complained of severe stomach pains. The doctor continued to treat him for malaria. When he finally died, that same doctor attributed his death to gastritis.

The sister of one of Bertha's previous patients, Margaret Stuhlfelder, fell ill, and the doctor suggested the parents call Bertha to help take care of her. By then, Bertha was wearing a white apron during her care visits and carrying a satchel containing her homemade elixirs. On examining the little girl, Bertha expressed her opinion that she had small chance of surviving. She remained at Margaret's bedside for three days while the girl suffered from stomach pain and vomiting. On February 28, 1921, she died of bronchopneumonia.

In December 1922, Bertha babysat three-year-old Beulah Pounds. She was the granddaughter of Sherman Pounds (Gene's cousin) who had died at the Gifford home in 1917. Her mother, Marguerite, was unwed but had a boyfriend who worked at the Gifford farm as a hired hand. Bertha and Marguerite often visited, so it was not unusual for her to leave the toddler with her "cousin." When Marguerite came to pick up Beulah on this occasion, the baby girl complained of stomach pain. Bertha convinced the mother to leave Beulah under her care, and by the next morning, she was dead. The cause of death, according to the doctor, was acute gastritis.

Finally, suspicion reared its head among the family of baby Beulah. The child's aunt found it odd that both her father and her niece had died while under the care of Bertha and that both had complained of stomach pain prior to their deaths. The aunt wanted an autopsy performed. The doctor refused to order an autopsy, and when the family was told that they would have to pay the costs to have a postmortem performed, they refused.

Bertha made it her business to attend every funeral in the surrounding area, but she did not attend baby Beulah's.

When a third Stuhlfelder child, seven-year-old Irene, fell ill with what her mother believed to be worms, the doctor treated her, and she began to get better. Bertha eventually came to help with the sick child, at which time, she grew worse and died. Still, the doctor did not question what had happened and attributed her death to an intestinal parasite. Mr. Stuhlfelder's mother also died while under Bertha's care in January 1926. At no time, the family told the *St. Louis Post-Dispatch* when they were interviewed at a later date, did they harbor any suspicion toward Bertha Gifford and the type of care she administered to their loved ones.

Gene and Bertha took in widower George Schamel and his two young sons in August 1925, soon after their mother and aunt had died. Both had died while under the care of Bertha. Seven-year-old Lloyd was ill when they moved in but grew sicker and died on August 11 of acute gastritis. Soon after, six-year-old Elmer also grew ill and died. At this point, the doctor finally became suspicious and ordered an autopsy. However, the father refused. Neighbors also started to talk at this time. Four members of the same family had died in a short time span, all under the care of Bertha Gifford, and the boys were so young. Bertha didn't help the situation when she insisted on talking about various murders and accidents to those neighbors with great enthusiasm.

During this time, Gene was having his own problems. With Prohibition in full swing, Gene had been making whiskey in the barn and had a partner selling it in nearby towns. When the men disagreed over money, Bertha chased the partner with a butcher knife, feeding the gossip mill further.

Despite the bad feeling between Gene and his partner, when the partner's seventy-two-year-old mother, Birdie Unnerstall, grew ill, Bertha was called in to nurse her. Birdie was elderly and had a heart condition, so when she died of chronic myocarditis, it wasn't surprising or suspicious.

On May 15, 1927, Bertha purchased more arsenic. On the same day, one of their farm workers, Ed Brinley, age forty-nine, was drinking when he passed out in their yard. Bertha fed him a ham sandwich, and he fell ill. When the doctor, the same doctor who had attended Bertha's past patients, arrived, he couldn't decide what might be wrong with the man. Brinley's mother visited, and while she was there, Bertha gave him a glass of lemonade and some water. When Ed's stomach pains grew worse, the doctor returned and called for a second opinion. The man died soon after the second doctor arrived, and the two medical experts could not agree on a cause of death. It was recorded as a disease that was unknown. Even then, no autopsy was ordered. Bertha and Gene even lent the Brinley family money to bury Ed Brinley.

By then, gossip had reached a fever pitch and finally reached the ears of prosecuting attorney Frank Jenny—and he listened. He called a grand jury in November 1927 to investigate Bertha and the mysterious deaths. Bertha was outraged. She threatened to sue anyone who spoke out against her for libel, and few took the chance. The Giffords moved to Eureka, Missouri, soon after.

Frank Jenny wasn't willing to give up that easily. In his investigation, he found Bertha had bought arsenic in unusually high amounts. He called a second grand jury, and more witnesses testified this time. Once the accusations against Bertha made the news, people called Jenny to tell him about patients who had died while under Bertha's care. He eventually had a list of seventeen deaths. The grand jury indicted Bertha Gifford for the deaths of two individuals: Ed Brinley and Elmer Schamel.

On August 25, 1928, Bertha's son James and granddaughter Ernestine were sitting outside, under a shady tree, trying to escape the heat. A car drove into the driveway of the house, and a man stepped out, asking if Mrs. Gifford was there. Jim went inside and fetched his mother. The man and Bertha spoke, then everyone went inside, and Ernestine followed her grandmother to her bedroom. Bertha powdered her face and rouged her cheeks, donned a hat and returned to speak to the man who turned out to be Andrew McDonnell, the police chief of Webster Groves, Missouri. Eventually, Bertha got in the car with McDonnell, and they departed. Chief McDonnell had not informed her that she was under arrest, only that he wanted to talk to her about the deaths of Ed Brinley and the Schamel boys. At that moment, Bertha was also unaware that the grand jury that had been called to look into her actions had concluded, and McDonnell's appearance and invitation were the results of their decision. She was fifty-six years old.

Chief McDonnell had a plan to get Bertha Gifford to talk. He invited her to sit in the front seat of the car with him on the ride, but he did not talk to her or to the judge who had accompanied him during the trip. The police officer's failure to ask her any questions or even initiate conversation made Bertha increasingly edgy. She finally spoke. She said she knew that her neighbors had been spreading lies about her and that she had been expecting a visit from the law. McDonnell simply told her they were almost at their destination. Bertha continued, asking if he planned to keep her in jail overnight. He told her that she could stay in his office if she liked. Once they arrived at the station, Chief McDonnell accompanied her to his office and pointed out a sergeant who was seated nearby. He told her to ask him if she needed anything. When Bertha wanted to know if he was going to question her, the police chief told her that he perhaps would later but that he had other things to do first. When Chief McDonnell returned that evening, Bertha insisted on talking about the case, telling him right off that she didn't give arsenic to "that Pounds child, now, that they made such a fuss over." She continued, "Believe me, Mr. McDonnell, I didn't give her any arsenic." Chief McDonnell then asked her, "Who did you give it to then?" Bertha's answer was a shocker, although the chief managed to maintain his poker face. "I gave it to Ed Brinley and the two Schamel boys," Bertha confessed. "I just put a little bit in their medicine…not enough to hurt them." And with that, Chief McDonnell left her again. The next morning, when he returned, she signed the following statement:

> *I, Bertha Gifford, wife of E.B. Gifford, now living at Eureka, Missouri, do make the following statement of my own free will without threats or promise of immunity on the part of Andrew McDonnell, Chief of Police of Webster Groves, or of F.W. Jenny, Prosecuting Attorney or of Sheriff Gorg of Franklin county that:*
>
> *My husband and I lived in the Nicholson place near Catawissa about Aug. 8, 1925, when George Schamel brought his son, Lloyd, about 8 or 9 years old, and his son, Elmer John, about 7 years old, to our house, where he and the boys made their home with us. Lloyd was sick at the time Dr. Hemker waited on him and left some medicine for him. I put*

> *some arsenic in the medicine before I gave it to him, and Lloyd died on or about August 11, 1925.*
>
> *About Sept. 18, 1925, Elmer John Schamel took sick. Dr. Hemker was called and left some medicine for him, and I put some arsenic in it, and Elmer John died about Sept. 22.*
>
> *About May 15, 1927, Edward Brinley, about 48 years old, drove up to our house in an old Ford. He was drunk. He came in, sat down for a little while, then got up and went out and fell down on the concrete walk.*
>
> *My husband went out and brought him in and fixed the bed for him in the front room, and my husband laid him on the bed. His mother came over and insisted we call a doctor. So, I called Dr. Hemker.*
>
> *He left some medicine for him, and I put some arsenic in the medicine. He died May 14, 1927. In all three cases, the patients were suffering from severe pains in the stomach, and I put arsenic in their medicine to quiet their pains.*

Gene Gifford, when he read the statement, refused to believe it. He posited that Bertha had a very nervous temperament and was rattled by being taken in for questioning. He hired a lawyer to represent his wife.

One very big question remained and was discussed freely among the area's gossips. What was Bertha Gifford's motive? Even Franklin County Sheriff Gorg had his doubts concerning her motive. He thought that perhaps Bertha attributed special healing powers to arsenic and believed it would help her patients.

Bertha finally realized what was at stake when she was returned to the Franklin County Jail. She wept and bemoaned the fact that her statement had been printed in newspapers. Besides refusing to eat, Bertha shouted at any reporters or photographers who tried to visit her. She continued to insist that she only gave the man and boys arsenic to ease their pains. While in jail, awaiting trial, her husband visited her every day. Her daughter, Lila, the mother of Ernestine, also visited Bertha one last time when she came to pick up the granddaughter her mother had been caring for. And that loving, caring grandmother's wish at that visit was to make sure Ernestine had a good winter coat. Bertha, as a grandmother, believed nothing was too good for her granddaughter.

When interviewed by the *St. Louis Post-Dispatch*, Dr. W.H. Hemker, who attended all the deaths, said he did not press for autopsies because he feared a libel suit. At the time of the interview, he supposed he had been wrong. Dr. James Stewart, the state health commissioner, weighed in, saying that the cause of death should be specific when filling out a death certificate, and if it is suspicious, the coroner should be called. He said, in the future, the State Board of Health would require a clear and concise cause of death; otherwise, the physician would be shirking his duty to both community and self.

The bodies of Ed Brinley, Elmer Schamel and Lloyd Schamel were exhumed and examined prior to Bertha's trial. Poison in sufficient amounts—enough to have caused their deaths—was found in the organs of the three people who had died under her care and to whom she had admitted to giving arsenic. At the inquest, Bertha's normally smiling and friendly husband, Gene, remained poker-faced and refused to talk to anyone.

Bertha Gifford's trial for the poisoning death of Ed Brinley commenced on November 19, 1928. She continued to maintain an appearance by coming into court with freshly bobbed hair and rouged cheeks. She wore a black coat with a brown fox collar, high-heeled shoes and gray silk stockings, according to the *St. Louis Post-Dispatch*. The largest visible difference in her appearance was that the once full-figured woman had lost a considerable amount of weight during her three months of incarceration.

At the trial, after prosecution witnesses testified to Brinley being cared for by Bertha, suffering from stomach pains and dying, as well as the finding arsenic in his body on exhumation, Bertha's attorneys mounted a defense of insanity to save her from death by hanging. Physicians examined the defendant and diagnosed "dementia praecox," which was characterized by her fascination with sick people, especially those on the precipice of death, and her morbid obsession with death and funerals.

The jury deliberated for three hours and twenty-six minutes, returning a verdict of not guilty "on the sole ground that she was insane at the time of the commission of the offense and has not recovered from such insanity." The time that was required to return the verdict was due to one juror contending that Bertha was insane at the time she poisoned Ed Brinley but had since recovered. No one voted for a verdict of guilty.

The question of Bertha's motive remained unanswered. Why did she kill these particular people when she helped many to recover? (Although the number who survived her ministrations is unknown.) There were whispers that perhaps she did it to ease the families' difficulties in the case of the drunkards and the motherless boys, for example. Could she have wanted the attention of the community by taking a near death patient—by her hand—and bringing them back to health? Or did she simply want the respect that came from generously caring from the sick? After all, she may have felt that she had lost that respect when she took up with a younger

Few photographs of Bertha Gifford still exist. This is a drawing of her in the courtroom during her trial for murder. *Courtesy of the* St. Louis Star-Times.

man while still married to Henry Graham (and she married that man soon after the death of her first husband). Graham's death is perhaps the one exception to Bertha's not wishing a fatal result after administering arsenic. She wanted to marry Gene Gifford, and she may have wanted the insurance money as well. There is a clear and defined motive behind that first death. But with the others, Bertha proclaimed she only wanted to do good, to help the sick.

Bertha Gifford was committed to Farmington State Hospital (no longer in existence) and spent the remaining twenty-three years of her life there. Her husband, Gene, visited her for a time, but when he found a new wife, the visits stopped. Her son James left the area soon after Bertha's commitment, and after a period of wandering, he settled in California. He never visited his mother and believed her to be guilty. Bertha Gifford died in 1951.

9.

A MASSACRE IN TOM'S TOWN

Kansas City Union Station, June 17, 1933

Chicago is the city most people think of when asked about mob violence and corruption during Prohibition and the Great Depression era. But during the same period, Kansas City had its own reputation as a wide-open city with rampant crime, gambling, prostitution and corruption that law enforcement did little to curb. It was "Tom's Town," ruled by political boss Tom Pendergast. Pendergast had an understanding with the underworld and, in particular, with Johnny Lazia, a hoodlum from the North Side who was also a big shot in Democratic politics who was said to control thousands of votes. But even this city was shaken by what happened on the morning of Saturday, June 17, 1933.

Frank "Jelly" Nash escaped from the federal penitentiary in Leavenworth, Kansas, in October 1930. He was lying low in one of gangland's favorite spots, Hot Springs, Arkansas, when, three years later, he was captured by two FBI agents, Frank Smith and Joseph Lackey, and by Muskogee, Oklahoma police chief Otto Reed. They notified Reed E. Vetterli, the FBI agent in charge of the Kansas City office, that they were returning with Nash on the 7:15 a.m. train and to meet them at Kansas City Union Station. Four of Nash's friends, Richard Galatas, Herbert Farmer, Louis Stacci and Frank Mulloy, were informed of his capture. They laid plans to free him when he arrived in Kansas City. They hired Verne Miller, a freelance gunman, for the effort. Miller went to Lazia to ask him for help in finding men to take on the job with him. Lazia declined to offer any of his men, but he put Miller in touch with Adam Richetti and his famous pal, Charles "Pretty Boy" Floyd.

Floyd began his criminal career in 1925 by robbing businesses in St. Louis. After knocking over several Kroger grocery stores, he and two others decided to make a larger score by robbing the company's payroll at its headquarters. The robbers escaped after a gun battle with the police. Floyd's companions were arrested, and they identified him as the third robber. He was called Pretty Boy for the first time in the newspapers in the September 18, 1925 edition of the *St. Louis Globe-Democrat*, although he may have already acquired the nickname from the hands at the oil rig where he worked due to his snappy dress. One of his biographers said that a witness to a Kroger robbery in St. Louis described him as "a mere boy—a pretty boy with apple cheeks," and the description stuck. However he got the name, Floyd hated it.

Floyd was sentenced to five years in the Missouri State Prison. He served thirty-nine months before being released. Just two days after getting out, Kansas City police arrested him for the first of twenty-nine times in 1929. He was not convicted in Missouri again, but he committed a string of crimes in Ohio and was sentenced to twelve to fifteen years in prison in 1930. He

Charles "Pretty Boy" Floyd (*left*) and the other men in this photograph were arrested and convicted of the robbery of Kroger's headquarters and grocery stores in St. Louis in 1925. *Courtesy of the Missouri Historical Society.*

escaped while being taken to prison and returned to Kansas City. During 1931 and 1932, Floyd robbed up to thirty banks in Oklahoma. Adam Richetti was a frequent fellow robber. Banks put up signs that read, "Notice to bank robbers: There is not enough cash in this bank to be worth the risk of robbing it." A banker was quoted as saying that if robbers held up his bank, "they'd have had to borrow money to get out of town."

Floyd and Richetti met Verne Miller almost by chance. The duo arrived in Kansas City on the night of June 16, after a bizarre trip across central Missouri and eastern Kansas. Their car was being repaired at a garage in Bolivar, Missouri, when Polk County sheriff Jack Killingsworth stopped to buy gas. The gangsters took the sheriff prisoner and drove to Osceola, where they dumped their car and stole another one. The trio drove to Ottawa and Paola, Kansas, and finally ended up in Kansas City. There, they left Killingsworth, unharmed, and drove away. Miller met Floyd and Richetti at Lazia's Club Paris to sign them up for the rescue attempt.

The next morning Miller, Floyd and Richetti parked in a green Plymouth in the lot just outside the door to Union Station. Nash, Smith, Lackey and Reed left the train. Vetterli, FBI agent Raymond J. Caffrey and Kansas City police officers W.J. "Red" Grooms and Frank Hermanson were waiting for them. They took Nash through the station in a phalanx.

Caffrey's car was parked near the green Plymouth. Caffrey unlocked the passenger door. It was a two-door sedan, so the front passenger seat had to be lowered for Lackey to climb in the back seat on the driver's side. Nash started to get in beside Lackey in the middle. Lackey told him to sit in the front seat, and so Nash slid into the driver's seat. Smith got in next to Lackey, and Reed sat on the right-hand passenger side in back. Grooms and Hermanson stood by the front passenger door, Vetterli next to them. Caffrey went behind his car and then to the driver's door.

The next sixty seconds were a blur. Two men stepped from behind the Plymouth, holding machine guns. There was a third man similarly armed behind Caffrey's car. One of the attackers shouted, "Up! Up! Up!" Then, "Let them have it!" The machine guns opened up. Grooms, Hermanson, Caffrey and Reed fell dead. Vetterli was hit in the left arm, and he scrambled to the back of the car. Lackey's shotgun was jammed between the driver's seat and the door post. He saw Nash lift his manacled hands above his head and duck. Nash shouted, "My God, don't shoot me!" He was then struck in the head and died. Reed was shot in the chest and died instantly. Lackey took three rounds, one from the front and two from the rear. Smith then bent down behind the front seat and pretended to be dead. He was unharmed.

Kansas City Union Station, circa 1930. *Courtesy of the Library of Congress.*

One of the gunmen came to the window, looked in and said, "He is dead. They are all dead in here." Vetterli made it inside the station to call for reinforcements, but it was too late. The attackers were gone after firing more than one hundred rounds.

The authorities began a massive manhunt, but Miller, Floyd and Richetti got away. On June 21, Floyd sent a postcard to authorities from Springfield, Missouri. In it, he said, "I—Charles Floyd—want it known that I did not participate in the massacre of officers in Kansas City."

Miller managed to elude the police for months, including escaping in a hail of bullets when he was surprised at his girlfriend's house in Chicago. In November 1933, his body was found in a ditch in Detroit. Authorities believed he was executed by underworld figures who blamed him for the intense FBI and police pressure that was put on all gangsters in an effort to find the killers.

Floyd and Richetti hid out in Buffalo, New York, for more than a year, undiscovered. When John Dillinger was killed by FBI agent Melvin Purvis in July 1934, the bureau named Pretty Boy Floyd Public Enemy Number One. In the meantime, the FBI developed evidence for any eventual trial of the killers. An informant, James Michael "Jimmy Needles" LaCapra, told them of Miller's meeting with Lazia in which he referred him to Floyd and Richetti. The Bureau finally broke Miller's girlfriend, who confirmed Jimmy Needles's story. All they needed then were the two remaining suspects.

Even criminals need to eat. Floyd and Richetti were not used to earning honest money, so they left their New York hideout to do what they did best—rob banks. They knocked over a bank in Tiltonsville, Ohio, and fled north to Wellsville, Ohio. There, the police spotted the duo the next day. After a gun battle, Richetti was captured, but Floyd got away. He wandered on foot to Mrs. Ellen Conkle's farm near East Liverpool, Ohio.

Melvin Purvis was in Cincinnati, working on a kidnapping, when he heard that Richetti was captured and Floyd had escaped. He got permission from J. Edgar Hoover to take a team of FBI agents to search for Pretty Boy. Purvis, three FBI agents, East Liverpool police chief Hugh McDermott, Deputy Chester Smith and two city officers conducted an intense search for the fugitive. They found him on the Conkle farm. Floyd ran across a corn field, but he was gunned down by Deputy Smith. As he lay dying, Floyd said, "I'm done for. You've hit me twice." Richetti was returned to Kansas City, where he was convicted of the murder of Frank Hermanson and executed in Missouri's gas chamber in 1938.

Johnny Lazia was convicted in federal court of income tax evasion. While out on bail, awaiting the results of his appeal, he went out for a night on the town with his wife. On their way home, Lazia's car, driven by his lieutenant and bodyguard, Big Charley Carollo, pulled into the driveway of the Park Central Hotel. Waiting there were gunmen who sprayed the car with machine gun fire. Lazia was mortally wounded. He died eleven hours later, wondering why anyone would shoot him, "the friend of everybody." It was later discovered that one of the machine guns that killed Lazia had been used in the Union Station Massacre. *Who would want Lazia killed?* We don't know because his slayers were never caught. We do know that Big Charley took over Lazia's enterprises. Jimmy Needles was alleged to be one of Lazia's killers, but he wasn't taken into custody because he was found dead on Long Island in August 1935. Galatas, Farmer, Stacci and Mulloy were convicted of conspiracy to cause the escape of a federal prisoner and received the maximum sentence of two years and a $10,000 fine.

That is the *official* story of the Kansas City Union Station Massacre, as told by the FBI. But wait—is that really what happened?

There is considerable doubt that Pretty Boy Floyd and Adam Richetti were the gunmen. (Everyone believes Verne Miller was there.) James "Blackie" Audette claimed that he drove Mary McElroy, the daughter of city manager and Pendergast crony Henry McElroy, to Union Station that morning because she had word that "all hell is going to break loose." Audette said the gunmen accompanying Miller were two local thugs, Homer and Maurice Denning, who had worked with Miller before. Others have suggested that they were Maurice Denning and William Weissman. At the time, some of the witnesses identified Harvey Bailey, a well-known Kansas City gangster, as one of the gunmen. Floyd, of course, denied that he took part in the shooting. But then again, he would, wouldn't he? No one knows for sure.

There are also doubts as to whether Miller and the two other gunmen, whoever they were, were trying to rescue Nash. Certainly, if that was their intent, they botched the job badly. And indeed, why would anyone trying to rescue a passenger in the car blast him away with machine guns almost as soon as he got in it?

There are even more serious doubts about who killed who. Professor Robert Unger obtained the entire FBI file on the Union Station Massacre through a Freedom of Information lawsuit. In analyzing the records, he concluded that only Red Grooms and Otto Reed were killed by the men wielding machine guns. He posits that Agent Lackey ended up with Chief

The aftermath of the Kansas City Union Station Massacre, showing the bodies of W.J. "Red" Grooms and Frank Hermanson lying next to the car on the left and showing a large hole in the windshield of the lawmen's car with the glass lying on the hood. *Courtesy of www.FBI.gov.*

Reed's pump action shotgun in the kerfuffle of taking Nash off the train and hustling him to the car. Reed's weapon, unbeknownst to Lackey, had been modified to fire when the rounds were pumped into the breech rather than when the trigger was pulled. When the bullets began to fly, Lackey, sitting in the rear seat behind Nash, raised the shotgun and pumped it, and the first round went into Nash's head. It also may have been the round that killed Caffrey, who was standing next to Nash outside the door. He pumped it again, and Officer Hermanson went down. The autopsies of the victims showed that Nash, Caffrey and Hermanson were not struck by machine gun bullets. And a famous photograph of the aftermath shows that the glass from windshield of the car was on the hood, indicating that the shot that had caused a large hole had come from *inside*, not outside, the car.

Unger claimed that this information was suppressed on the order of J. Edgar Hoover to avoid making Lackey—and the FBI—look terrible. Hoover used the Union Station Massacre and the FBI's role in its aftermath as a weapon to entice additional power and prestige for the bureau.

10.

THE MORTIMER MURDER

Mexico, Missouri, is a town of about twelve thousand citizens in central Missouri. In 1937, it reigned as the firebrick capital of the world when its A.P. Green Fire Brick Company became the largest firebrick maker in the world. And A.P. Green's was not the only brick factory in town; a competitor, Mexico Refractories, had opened in 1929. These two companies helped carry the town through the ups and downs of the Great Depression. Murder was certainly never considered a possibility as residents approached the holidays in 1937.

Margaret Mortimer (Peggy to her family) spent the afternoon before Thanksgiving at the beauty parlor and shopping around Mexico's downtown square. She visited with friends in front of Scott's Store, browsed and made a purchase in Pilcher's Jewelry Store, shopped at Marlowe's Drug Store and bought magazines at the Gentle News Agency. She lived with her husband, A.S. "Bert" Mortimer, in the former home of the president of the defunct Hardin College, which was then owned by her parents, Mr. and Mrs. B.F. Rhodus. The family had visitors from California, a Mr. and Mrs. James Irwin, staying with them for the holiday. Margaret was a forty-two-year-old musician and singer who performed at concerts across the state, as well as in amateur theatricals. Her husband of nineteen years worked at Continental Bank Supply, her father's company. The couple had lived in Mexico for eleven years. The family was socially prominent in the town and state and had many powerful friends, including the governor of Missouri, Lloyd C. Stark. Margaret was described as "one of Mexico's most prominent and charming women."

Right: Margaret Mortimer often performed as a soloist at local churches across the state. *Courtesy of the Audrain County Historical Society.*

Below: Margaret Mortimer lived only steps away from the scene of the crime with her husband, Bert, and her parents. The house was the former home of the president of the shuttered Hardin College, which was located across the street. *Courtesy of the Audrain County Historical Society.*

Margaret left downtown as darkness fell, walking the seven blocks home. She crossed the railroad tracks with Ama Potts, a sixteen-year-old girl who worked at the drugstore, following about half a block behind her. When they reached the block before the Rhodus home at approximately 6:15 p.m., Ama passed her. Moments later, the girl heard a woman scream once, a second muffled scream and then three thuds. Ama ran home, frightened.

Those screams had come from Margaret. Someone had grabbed her from behind. She screamed once before hands were placed over her mouth as she tried to scream a second time. She was struck across the side of the head and face, then harder on the back of the head, rendering her unconscious. Her assailant grabbed her ankles tightly and dragged her to the rear of a nearby home that was undergoing renovation, leaving a trail of her shoes, hat and a blood-soaked handkerchief along the way. From the condition of the woman's clothing, investigators surmised the perpetrator pushed her dress over her head, fur coat up under her arms and tore off her underwear before being scared away.

At the same time, Mr. Irwin, who was staying at the Rhodus home, came outside to move his automobile around to the garage in the back of the house. He had trouble opening the garage door and left his car running, the headlamps casting light toward the abandoned house where the crime was being committed. This may have been what scared the attacker away before completing a further assault on Margaret.

At the Rhodus home, the family felt it was unusual for Margaret to be absent for a meal. They believed her to be out with nieces or practicing for a scheduled musical performance that was coming up. So, at 7:10 p.m., they sat down to eat dinner. For an hour and a half, Margaret laid in a pool of her own blood behind the vacant house in sight of her family home, dying from her head wounds.

The owners of the vacant house, the Holtmans, came by around 7:45 p.m. to show their son, who was back from college for the holidays, the progress of work that was being done. They entered through the front and were checking a porch when Mr. Holtman heard moans coming from outside the house. He used his flashlight to find the source of the moans and located what he believed to be a half-naked male body. He sent his son to a nearby house to call the police, then waited for them to arrive, making no further investigation. He also hailed three young boys who were passing by and asked them to go to the Rhodus home and ask Bert to come help. As he walked across the Holtmans' lawn, Bert saw the fallen hat and recognized it as his wife's. He fell to his knees beside her and tried to wipe the blood from

The Holtman house was the scene of Margaret Mortimer's murder. The assailant hid behind a tree as she approached and then attacked Margaret from behind. After knocking the woman unconscious, the assailant dragged her behind the vacant house, preparing to attack her further until he was frightened away. *Courtesy of the Audrain County Historical Society.*

her face. Mortimer covered her with her coat to protect her from the cold, and he called for a blanket to put over her while they awaited the ambulance. The police arrived at around the same time as the victim's husband.

At the hospital, the doctor examined Margaret's three head wounds: one across the top of her skull that resulted in a fracture, one at the back of her head and one along the side of her head that caused a black eye and a broken nose. Margaret died without regaining consciousness as a result of the skull fracture and loss of blood. Because of the amount of blood at the scene, one thing the police looked for was anyone with blood-stained clothing or discarded clothing that was stained by blood.

Bloodhounds were called in from nearby Fulton, Missouri, but due to the trampled nature of the grounds surrounding the attack by interested bystanders, they were unable to follow a scent. The police immediately engaged the services of the Missouri State Highway Patrol. There was no sign of robbery. The victim still wore an expensive bracelet and her engagement and wedding rings. The family said they'd received no threats, nor did Margaret have any known enemies.

One line of investigation involved tying this attack to two prior attacks on women in Mexico. On November 4, 1936, only one year earlier, Helen Fray Palmer, a twenty-six-year-old elementary school teacher, was coming home from the movie theater when she was struck on the head from behind within a hundred yards of where Margaret's attack occurred. The attacker grabbed her and tore her clothing. She fought the man, bit him on the hand and screamed for help. He fled before Palmer had a chance to notice any details of his appearance beyond the fact he wore a tan overcoat. The young teacher required three stitches to close the wound in her head.

Miss Louise Leslie, a twenty-nine-year-old stenographer, required six stitches for a wound to her head after an assailant attacked her in April 1937. On her way home from work, she heard footsteps behind her. She started to look around when she reached a streetlight, but the attacker grabbed her by the throat, struck her with something heavy and pushed her into a ditch. She, too, screamed and scared the man away. The only details Miss Leslie gave were that the man was medium-sized and wore overalls and a suit coat. Neither woman was able to determine whether her attacker was Black or white.

A third woman, Mary Helmich, also reported being chased by a man. He came out of the deserted Hardin College grounds, across the street from where Margaret was later killed, and pursued Helmich, who escaped by running to her sister's home nearby. She had nothing to add to the suspect's description.

Bert Mortimer did report passing a "negro dressed in a cap and brown checked coat" near the scene of the crime as he walked home on South Jefferson Street between 5:30 p.m. and 5:50 p.m. The man "watched him intently" as they met and passed at a street corner. The suspect was believed to be at least six foot two inches tall and husky. Bert had never seen the man before. Early on, the police focused on trying to locate the man who fit this description. The police chief said a piece of white oak firewood, fifteen inches long and three inches in diameter, was suspected to be the murder weapon. The wood piece was found lying in the driveway during a search for clues. That wood piece and magazines collected at the scene were taken to highway patrol headquarters to be tested for fingerprints.

Governor Stark immediately offered a $300 reward for the conviction of the killer of Margaret Mortimer. He called it "one of the most brutal and shocking in the state's history" and also urged law enforcement to double their efforts to find the murderer. The *Mexico Ledger*, the local newspaper, headed an effort to build a reward fund large enough to encourage someone to come forward with information. Only one day into the effort, the fund exceeded the $1,000 mark.

Sixty hours after the murder, law enforcement was no closer to finding the person who attacked Margaret. The firewood that had been found in the driveway the night of the crime was determined to be the murder weapon. It had been taken from a nearby wood pile and carried to the spot where Margaret was assaulted. The investigators did say that they believed the man who was responsible to be a sex maniac because, in the three attacks on women in Mexico, no attempt was made to rob them.

On the Saturday following the murder, Margaret's purse, which had been missing since the murder, was found empty by a young paper carrier taking a shortcut across the lawn of a nearby vacant home. This led Colonel Marvin Casteel, the head of the Missouri State Highway Patrol, to declare that the murder of Margaret Mortimer was a crime with "both sex and robbery motives." A small parcel containing deodorant still wrapped in the paper from the Marlowe Drug Store was also discovered nearby. However, six silver teaspoons that had been purchased at Pilcher's Jewelry Store that day were not in the purse (where the staff of the jewelry store remembered seeing Margaret place them after her purchase). There was also no money in the purse. Margaret's right-hand glove was also missing.

The SHP planned to prepare and issue a poster of the man that Bert Mortimer saw on his way home around the time that his wife was attacked. Casteel said the murderer may have been a transient and that they were continuing to look for "suspicious negro characters," although they were "by no means sure that the murderer was a negro." Court records of all the men from Audrain County who had been convicted of a sex crime in the past twenty years were also investigated. The SHP tried to ascertain the location of all former sex offenders who had been in state prison. Even men who had been convicted of lesser crimes against women and those who had been charged but not convicted were investigated to no avail.

Finding no trace of Margaret's murderer, local law enforcement "borrowed" Lieutenant Ira Cooper from the St. Louis Police Department (the same Ira Cooper who, as a journalist, wrote about Frankie and Johnny). Lieutenant Cooper was born and lived in Mexico before beginning his highly esteemed career as a police detective in St. Louis. Cooper was one of the highest-ranking Black police officers in the United States and had been recognized nationally and internationally for his success as a detective. This was not the first time Lieutenant Cooper had helped Audrain County and Mexico officials solve particularly thorny criminal situations. Cooper

ABLE

—Sid Whiting Photo

Sergeant Ira L. Cooper, the only Negro Officer of the rank in St. Louis, and so far as is known, west of the Mississippi river.

Lieutenant Ira Cooper was a renowned detective in his day, receiving accolades from as far away as Scotland Yard. He was the first Black detective and lieutenant in the St. Louis Police Department. He was born in Audrain County and had a knowledge of the citizens of Mexico, Missouri, that, when combined with his policing skills, made him an ideal candidate for investigating Margaret Mortimer's murder. Unfortunately, he did not keep written notes or share his observations, and although he said he had leads on the killer, he grew ill and died before closing the case. *Courtesy of the Mercantile Library at the University of Missouri–St. Louis.*

was also responsible for solving prominent St. Louis cases. His method was, when looked at on the surface, fairly obvious. He was widely acquainted in the local African American community and kept his ears open to gossip, which often gave him the information he needed to solve crimes. He returned to St. Louis after investigating the Mortimer murder and fell ill and died. Lieutenant Cooper worked alone and did not keep written records of his investigations. No one knew whether or not he had uncovered anything useful in Mexico.

Law enforcement officials were inundated with letters offering clues and information regarding the murder. Most of the letters were considered to be from "cranks." One of the letters suggested looking at an empty firebrick kiln at the edge of the city, where "hoboes" gathered. Police said that was one of the first places they had searched, and they said they had questioned all present—to no avail. One suspect, who was said to resemble the description given of the Black man seen by Bert Mortimer on the evening of his wife's murder, was brought to Mexico, but Mortimer said he was not the man.

In an interview with a reporter from the *St. Louis Star and Times* newspaper, Bert Mortimer, who was then fifty-two years old, described his life with Margaret. They were married almost twenty years, and he said, "We never had a single quarrel all our married life, not even a lovers' spat." He and Margaret moved to Mexico from New York City, where Bert had run a successful law practice. In Mexico, he joined his father-in-law's business, Continental Bank Supply Co., as office manager. He and his wife were active in civic affairs from the time they moved to town. Bert was active in Boy Scouts, Rotary Club and the chamber of commerce. He was a staunch Democrat and considered Governor Stark a close friend. He was also a friend of former New York governor Alfred E. Smith. He and Margaret met in Atlantic City after being introduced by a mutual friend. Margaret was living there at the time with her mother, whose health was poor. After a two-year courtship, they were married in a Catholic church, Bert's religious preference. Margaret remained a lifelong Methodist. They moved to her parents' home in Mexico, but only after Margaret had spent an extended amount of time there and convinced her husband to join her. They were the subject of much gossip during this "separation," which Bert said had no basis in reality. Their lack of children was a disappointment, however.

On December 2, one week after Margaret's murder, Colonel Casteel announced that the investigation had ended, although they would continue to search out leads from patrol headquarters. Casteel's final hope was to find a possible suspect using fingerprints on objects that had been found near the scene. The next day, December 3, 1937, an investigation was opened into the death of another Mexico resident, William E. Baise. Baise, a Black man, was found dead by his nine-year-old daughter; he had a gunshot wound on his head and a shotgun at his feet when he was found in his residence on the deserted Hardin College campus. His death was ruled a suicide. Baise had been an unemployed farmhand, and according to his wife's employer, Forrest Noel, he had been depressed because of the lack of work. Baise had been questioned several times about Margaret's murder, contributing to that depression. Noel said that Baise came to him worried about the questioning he had undergone and wanting to return to the farm he had come from in Callaway County. Yet, he was worried that if he left town, he would be even more suspect in the murder. Noel made an appointment the next day to take Baise to inquire about work on the repaving of Mexico's streets. Baise never showed.

Baise's fingerprints were taken to check against those that had been found on articles at the scene of Margaret's death. At the inquest, Baise was eliminated as a suspect, and both of his children testified that he was at home from the time they arrived after school until bedtime. Police said Baise was never a suspect in the murder, and his questioning was routine.

Local law enforcement continued to investigate any information that came their way with no result. By the end of December, the reward fund had reached over $3,000. That reward was never claimed.

In a final twist, Bert Mortimer went missing on August 29, 1953, after he boarded a train headed for New York City to attend a funeral for a family member. Bert never attended that funeral. Finally, in October, Mexico police were notified that Bert had collapsed on the streets of New York and had been taken to a hospital, where he died without regaining consciousness. He was buried in the city cemetery. His family later had his body exhumed, identified him and reburied him in their family plot in New York.

Margaret's murderer was never identified.

11.

"WHY DID YOU HAVE TO SHOOT HIM?"

The Kidnapping and Murder of Bobby Greenlease

The tragedy of the kidnapping and murder of Bobby Greenlease unfolded with what today would be regarded as amazing speed. Less than ninety days after the crime, the perpetrators, Carl Austin Hall and Bonnie Brown Heady, were caught, convicted and executed. But the story lingered for years, not only in the hearts of the Greenlease family, but in the minds of the public. Hall claimed that they spent hardly any of the $600,000 in ransom money. He said the police took it all when he was arrested, but over half of it had disappeared by the time it was booked into evidence, and it has never been accounted for.

Carl Austin Hall came from a solid family. His father was a successful attorney in Pleasanton, Kansas. Hall attended the Kemper Military School in Boonville, Missouri, for three years. One of his classmates was Paul Greenlease, the son of Robert Greenlease, a wealthy Kansas City car dealer. Hall joined the Marines in 1938 and reenlisted in 1942. When not in combat, he was a disciplinary problem, getting drunk and going AWOL. But he fought at Peleliu and Okinawa, two of the Marines' toughest battles, and was awarded two bronze stars for his bravery. After the war, Hall's mother died (his father had died in 1932), leaving him $200,000 in cash, stocks and bonds and 1,170 acres of prime farmland. By 1951, he had squandered it all on booze and high living. Hall didn't want to work, so he decided to raise money in another way. Hall bought a pistol and began living a life of petty crime, robbing cab drivers. Unfortunately for his criminal career, he wasn't very good at it. He went to prison in Jefferson City for fifteen months after taking only $33 off his victim. While in his cell, he had dreams of making a big strike that would set him up for life. In his dreams, he would kidnap a rich kid, and that kid was Bobby Greenlease. Hall was released from prison in April 1953.

Bonnie Brown Heady was the daughter of prosperous farmers in northwest Missouri. She married Vernon Heady, a livestock merchant, but it was not a happy union. Vernon did not want children, and Bonnie said she had eleven abortions during their married life. Life outside the home was better for her. Heady was an accomplished horsewoman (she won a prize for being the best-dressed cowgirl) and bred pedigreed boxer dogs. After she divorced Vernon in 1952, Heady fell on hard times. She took to making money as a prostitute. Her life was changed (and shortened) when she met Hall at a bar in St. Joseph.

In June 1953, Hall revealed his plan to Heady—or at least most of it. He planned to kill the boy from the beginning, because, as he said later, "He's evidence." Heady said she only found out about that part the day before they kidnapped him. For most of September 1953, Hall and Heady watched the family. Hall bought a bag of lime, a .38 revolver, stationery for the ransom notes and prepaid envelopes. Hall decided that they would ask for $600,000 in $10 and $20 bills because that would fit in a duffel bag and not weigh too much. He planned to demand that the bills come from all twelve Federal Reserve banks so that it would be harder to track the serial numbers.

On September 28, all was ready. They parked outside the exclusive French Institute of Notre Dame de Sion and watched as Robert Greenlease dropped off his six-year-old son, Bobby. Hall and Heady drove to a nearby Katz Drugstore parking lot, where Hall waited. Heady took a cab to the school. She rang the bell. The mother superior was out that day, and her second in command, Mother Marthanna, was teaching a class. Sister Morand answered the door. Heady told her that she was Virginia Greenlease's sister and that Bobby's mother had a heart attack and wanted him to come to the hospital. Heady's nervous demeanor and the unusual request did not arouse suspicions in Sister Morand. She fetched Bobby out of class. "He was so trusting," Heady said later.

The two of them returned to the Katz Drugstore parking lot and got into Hall's car. They told Bobby they were going to get ice cream before seeing his dad. Instead, Hall drove into Kansas. The trio stopped on a farm road. Heady had her dog with her, so she left the car and took the dog down the road. Hall went to the passenger side of the car and climbed in beside Bobby. Hall tried to strangle Bobby, but the rope was too short. Bobby kicked

Bobby and Robert Greenlease. *Courtesy of the St. Louis Mercantile Library at the University of Missouri–St. Louis.*

and screamed. Hall threw Bobby to the floor and, while holding him down with both feet, hit him with the butt of his .38 revolver. When that didn't quiet the boy, he shot him in the head, killing him instantly. Hall wrapped Bobby's body in a plastic sheet.

"Why did you have to shoot him?" Heady asked. "I thought you were going to strangle him."

"I tried to, but the goddamned rope was too short. Goddamn it, he was fighting and kicking. I had to shoot him."

They took the body to Heady's house in St. Joseph and buried it in a crude grave in the backyard after pouring lime on it. Then, Hall returned to Kansas City to send the first of several ransom letters.

When Mother Marthanna left her class, she found that Bobby was gone. She called the Greenlease residence and spoke to Virginia. The alarm was raised. Robert Greenlease called the Kansas City police chief, who alerted the FBI because if the kidnappers had crossed state lines, they would have violated the Lindbergh Kidnapping Law. The kidnapping was publicly announced at 3:00 p.m. It was front-page news in Kansas City by the next day and in the national headlines a day after that.

The first ransom letter was received by special delivery at 6:00 p.m. on September 28. Hall demanded $600,000, divided into $400,000 in $20 bills and $200,000 in $10 bills. The money was to be packed into a duffel bag. Hall, who signed the letter with "M," promised to give directions for turning over the ransom in a future letter. Hall sent a second letter with a medal he had taken from Bobby's body. He called the Greenlease residence to make sure the second letter was received and that the ransom was being assembled from the various Federal Reserve banks.

Over the next few days, Hall sent more letters with elaborate instructions for finding directions for the ransom drop (a note was to be taped under mailboxes and on a certain car in a used car lot). Hall seemed to enjoy playing the hide-and-seek game with the family. Finally, Robert Ledterman, the family's representative in dealing with the kidnappers, told Hall on a telephone call, "This idea of climbing the trees and looking in a bird's nest for a note, then climbing on your belly somewhere looking for something under a rock with a red-white-and-blue ribbon around it—that's getting tiresome. You know, you and I don't have to play ball that way. We can deal man to man."

At last, on the night of October 4, a successful drop was made in rural Jackson County. Hall called and said he had the money. He told Ledterman that the boy was well and that he would send a telegram to Pittsburg, Kansas, with instructions on where to find him. Ledterman immediately left for Pittsburg.

Hall and Heady drove all night and arrived in St. Louis on the morning of October 5. Hall bought a green metal footlocker and a black metal suitcase and stuffed the ransom money in them. They wandered around town until they finally rented an apartment across the street from Tower Grove Park. Hall left Heady there and called a cab. He put the footlocker and suitcase in the cab and told the cabbie he wanted a call girl. The driver put him in touch with another cab driver named John Hager. Hager worked for Ace Cab, a company owned by mobster Joseph Costello. Hall transferred the footlocker and suitcase to Hager's cab.

Hager hooked Hall up with a prostitute named Sandy O'Day. He took them to the Coral Court Motel in St. Louis County. The next day, Hall told

Hager to put O'Day on a plane to Los Angeles, where he wanted her to mail a letter to a St. Joseph lawyer of Hall's acquaintance in a harebrained scheme to establish an alibi. When they were alone, O'Day told Hager, "This guy is loaded with dough. He opened one of the suitcases, and there must be a million dollars in it." While Hager was gone, Hall rented a car and bought a garbage can, plastic bags and shovel. He spent the day driving around St. Louis County, looking for a place to bury the loot, but he failed to find a suitable spot.

Hager told his boss, Costello, that he suspected that Hall might be the Greenlease kidnapper. Costello called Lieutenant Louis A. Shoulders of the St. Louis Police Department, whom he may have worked shakedowns with in the past. After Hall's unsuccessful hunt for a hiding place for the ransom money, Hager took him to an apartment at the Town House Hotel in the Central West End in St. Louis. Hall lugged the footlocker and suitcase full of money up to the third-floor room.

At around 7:30 p.m. on October 6, Shoulders and Patrolman Elmer Dolan burst into Hall's room. They searched the room, took the key to the footlocker and suitcase Hager and O'Day had mentioned and found them in the closet. Hall also had a briefcase with about $20,000 in it. Shoulders looked in the briefcase and said, "You've got a lot of money there, haven't you?" Hall replied, "Yes, a little bit." Shoulders said, "I'm going to put the briefcase back where I found it. I want you to notice that."

Shoulders left the room. According to author John Heidenry, Joseph Costello was waiting in the hall. Shoulders and Dolan arrested Hall and left with the briefcase for the police station. They left the footlocker and suitcase in the apartment. As they were leaving, Hall saw a third man—almost certainly Costello—in the hallway. Hall was booked in the Newstead Street station at 8:57 p.m. on October 6, nine days after he killed Bobby Greenlease. Shoulders and Dolan left the station, supposedly for personal errands. What happened next is a matter of dispute.

Shoulders and Dolan said they brought the footlocker and metal suitcase to the police station, but no one there backed their story. What really happened was that Shoulders, Dolan, Hager and Costello had met at Costello's house. They took the footlocker to his basement and spread the money on a table. Some, but not all, of the money was put back. A later count by the FBI showed that $296,280 was recovered; $303,720 was missing. Shoulders and Dolan managed to sneak the footlocker and suitcase into Shoulders's office at the police station. Hall confessed to the kidnapping but said that Bobby was killed by a man named Tom Marsh, sending the authorities on a chase

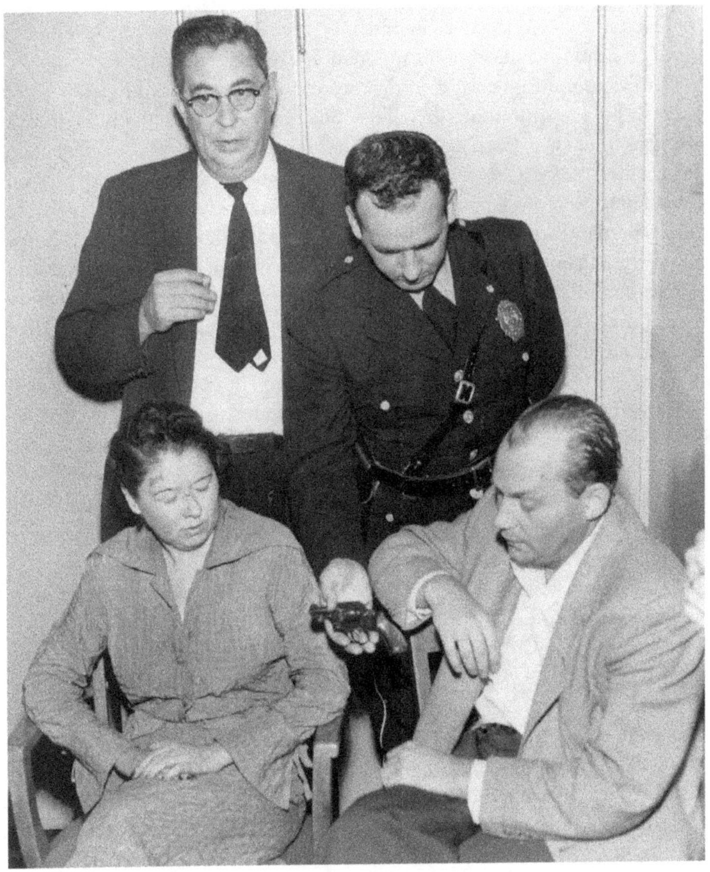

Lieutenant Louis A. Shoulders and Patrolman Elmer Dolan with Bonnie Heady and Carl Austin Hall. This image was taken shortly after Heady and Hall's capture on October 8, 1953. Dolan is holding the revolver that was used to kill Bobby Greenlease. *Courtesy of the St. Louis Mercantile Library at the University of Missouri–St. Louis.*

after a phantom. They asked about the woman, and he told them where to find Heady. She was arrested the next morning. The FBI found Bobby's body later that day. The St. Louis Police Department searched unsuccessfully for the missing ransom money. The authorities eventually decided that "Tom Marsh" was a fiction. Finally, on October 10, Hall and Heady made a full confession. Two weeks later, Shoulders, under intense suspicion, attempted to resign from the force, but his resignation was refused.

In this case, the wheels of justice ground rapidly. Hall and Heady were indicted by a federal grand jury. They pleaded guilty, and in a brief trial, a jury gave them the death penalty on November 18. They were sentenced to be executed on December 18, 1953, in the Missouri State Prison in Jefferson City. There were no lengthy appeals. In the time between their sentencing and its implementation, authorities interviewed Hall and demanded to know about the missing money. Hall insisted that it was all in the footlocker and suitcase and that he did not hide any of it anywhere. That didn't keep treasure hunters from looking for an elusive bag of money that was supposedly buried somewhere in St. Louis County.

Missouri governor Phil Donnelly was swamped with requests for tickets to watch the execution, but he pointed out that it was a federal, not a state, execution. (The federal government had no facilities for the executions and contracted with the State of Missouri to carry them out.) On the appointed day, Hall and Heady were led to the gas chamber. They were blindfolded and put into two chairs, side-by-side. Pellets containing sodium cyanide were dropped into vats of sulfuric acid, creating cyanide gas. Eighty-one days after Hall and Heady kidnapped and murdered Bobby Greenlease, they were dead.

Shoulders and Dolan were indicted for perjury for lying about bringing the suitcases to the police station when they arrested Hall. Shoulders was convicted and sentenced to three years in prison. Dolan was convicted and sentenced to two years. Costello was convicted of an unrelated federal crime. Both Shoulders and Costello died of heart attacks in 1962. After their deaths, Dolan admitted to the FBI that Shoulders had given Costello half the ransom money before taking Hall to the police station. President Lyndon Johnson pardoned Dolan in 1965. He died in 1973. Robert Greenlease died in 1969, and Bobby's mother, Virginia, died in 2001 at the age of ninety-one. Shoulders's son Louis Jr. was involved in mob activities in St. Louis. He was murdered in a car bombing in the Ozarks in 1972. Shoulders's granddaughter Susan was a heroin addict. Her body was found at a St. Louis recycling center, where it had been crushed by a trash compactor. She had apparently fallen asleep in a dumpster.

The ransom money that was recovered was returned to the Greenlease family. Of the missing money, only $1,690 ever turned up. No one knows what happened to the rest.

12.

THE UNLUCKIEST TOWN IN AMERICA

The Killings of Ken McElroy and Bobbi Jo Stinnett

Just about everyone who lived in or near the town of Skidmore in northwest Missouri would tell you that Ken McElroy was a bully—even more than that, he was a criminal who terrorized the citizens and defied law enforcement for years. But no one in the crowd of more than sixty who were present when McElroy died would tell you who pulled the trigger of the rifle that shot him to death on July 10, 1981.

As a teenager, Kenneth Rex McElroy was a good-looking kid. He was muscular, with dark hair and what the girls called pretty, dark-blue eyes. They called him "Kenny," as did most of his friends. In his mid-teens, Kenny discovered that he could make money stealing things—so long as he didn't get caught. He started off small, a hog or two here and there, and as he got older, he moved on to more serious crimes. McElroy expanded his operations in northwest Missouri and northeast Kansas to become the leader of a ring of thieves, stealing livestock, grain and farm chemicals. Law enforcement knew who he was and what he was doing, but they couldn't make a case.

Kenny liked girls, or perhaps more accurately, he liked sex. There were rumors that he raped a young girl in Quitman. He married for the first time in 1952, at the age of eighteen. About five years later, he shot a fifteen-year-old girl named Sharon during an argument. Fearing prosecution, McElroy demanded a divorce from his first wife so that he could marry Sharon, thus crippling any case against him for assault. It wouldn't be the only time he resorted to such a tactic.

McElroy hired Richard "Gene" McFadin as his lawyer to defend him against a charge of felony assault when he shot the stepfather of one of his girlfriends. Ultimately, the case was dropped, apparently for the lack of a key witness. McFadin racked up his first victory in a ten-year relationship with a client who had a knack for shooting people. With McFadin's help, McElroy also showed a knack for wriggling out of trouble. In 1972, he was charged with four counts of felony theft of hogs in Andrews County. The cases were dismissed when the witnesses against him recanted their statements.

In 1973 and 1974, McElroy faced his most serious criminal prosecution yet. McElroy took up with Trena McCloud when she was twelve. She had a baby by him when she was only fourteen. When Trena tried to flee McElroy, he grabbed her, went to Trena's parents' house with his shotgun, set their house on fire and shot their dog on the way back to his truck, all while Trena watched. Fortunately, her parents were not home at the time. He was charged with child molestation, rape and arson.

McElroy turned once again to McFadin. Gene McFadin was a master of an art that is little known or appreciated outside of the legal profession, but one that is essential to the successful practice of law: the art of obtaining the continuance. First, he asked the court to transfer the cases against McElroy to different counties in northwest Missouri. Then, he came up with numerous reasons why the cases weren't ready for trial. And these delays allowed McElroy to use his own methods of defeating the charges—making sure the potential witnesses didn't testify. The key witness was Trena McCloud. As he had done to avoid prosecution for shooting Sharon, he obtained a divorce and married Trena to confound any prosecution in his pending criminal case. McFadin provided a signed affidavit from Trena, recanting all of her prior statements against McElroy. As a practical matter, the cases had to be dropped.

McElroy was seemingly impervious to enforcement of the law, no matter how violent or egregious his conduct was in private or in public. That belief of the citizens of Skidmore was reinforced by his next serious brush with the criminal justice system.

On July 22, 1976, McElroy shot Skidmore farmer Romaine Henry in the stomach and face for no apparent reason. The state charged McElroy with assault with intent to kill. McFadin once again worked his legal magic to transfer the case out of Nodaway County, where the crime occurred, to Gentry County for trial. He also obtained continuances that postposed the trial to August 25, 1977. While the case was pending, McElroy cruised slowly by the Henry farm more than one hundred times or stopped and pretended to work on the truck's engine with the hood up until he slammed it shut and peeled out, spewing gravel. At trial, Henry was adamant about what happened, but McFadin, unable to shake him on that, went after him for failing to mention a thirty-year-old conviction Henry had for a fistfight, for which he paid a ten-dollar fine. Prosecution witnesses placed McElroy near the Henry farm at the time of the shooting, but McElroy testified that he was home all day. McFadin came up with two witnesses from Iowa who backed him up. McElroy was acquitted.

The road to McElroy's death began on April 25, 1980, when he squabbled with Lois Bowenkamp over whether one of his children tried to take some candy from her store without paying for it. That evening Ken, Trena and their daughter Tammy drove slowly by the Bowenkamps' home, starting days of harassment. McElroy and Trena drove by the house on multiple occasions, displaying weapons. Law enforcement did nothing.

On the evening of July 8, 1980, Ken McElroy was drinking at the D&G Tavern, the local Skidmore watering hole owned by Del and Greg Clement. Across an alley from the tavern was the back of the Bowenkamp store. Bo Bowenkamp, Lois's husband, returned to the store after it closed to see a repairman about the air conditioner. He took a knife from the meat counter and cut up cardboard boxes to put on the loading dock in the back, where the electrician could work. McElroy drove up in his pickup truck, parked next to the dock and got out. McElroy and Bo had words. Bo finally said, "This is private property you know. And we want you off of it." McElroy said, "Nobody tells me what to do." Bo was inside the store when McElroy returned to the loading dock with a shotgun. Bo jerked his head to the right just as McElroy fired. He was hit on the left side of his neck. A boy saw Bo bleeding profusely inside the back door and rushed to the tavern, hollering, "The old man's been shot!" Two men went for Marshal Dave Dunbar, and another called an ambulance. Dunbar asked Bo who had shot him. "Ken McElroy," he said. Dunbar found bloodstains three feet inside the door and shotgun pellets in the ceiling. Bo was rushed to the hospital, where once again he identified McElroy as the person who shot him. Bo survived.

McElroy was charged with felony assault in the first degree. Gene McFadin went to work. McElroy was released on bail. He showed up at the D&G in Skidmore the next day, joking about "the commotion" at the grocery store the night before. The customers were aghast. Marshal Dunbar wondered if he had broken out of jail.

McFadin filed his usual motion for change of venue, and the case was transferred to Harrison County. While out on bail, McElroy threatened a

Ken McElroy was killed outside the D&G Tavern in Skidmore, Missouri, which is shown here as it appears today. *Photograph by Reuben Hemmer.*

woman, her ex-husband and their children in St. Joseph with a shotgun during an act of road rage. His bail was not revoked. When taken to trial on the charge of brandishing the weapon in December 1980, the driver and her ex-husband recanted their prior statements. McElroy was acquitted.

At last, on June 25, 1981, the trial of Kenneth McElroy for the shooting of Bo Bowenkamp began. McFadin had to call McElroy to testify because he was claiming self-defense, but he had another witness he (or most likely McElroy) dug up—a woman from Iowa who claimed she just happened to be there when Bo supposedly threatened McElroy with a knife. Coincidentally (or perhaps not), she was the daughter-in-law of one of McElroy's alibi witnesses in the Romaine Henry trial.

The principal factual issue was where Bo was standing when he got shot. Bo said he was inside the door, and McElroy said he was on the loading dock with a knife. The physical evidence supported Bo. His blood pool was entirely inside the door. The shotgun pellets in the ceiling could not have been there unless the target of the blast was inside the door.

The jury struggled a bit but settled on a verdict of guilty of second-degree assault. Under Missouri law, in this type of case, the jury sets the punishment. The maximum penalty was five years, but the jury set McElroy's sentence at just two years. Only afterward were they told

McElroy's history by the deputy in charge of the jury, and they were not happy to find out that they had gone far too easy on the defendant. McElroy was released on bond, and just as he had done in August, he was back in the D&G in Skidmore the same day.

Although the jury returned a verdict, the case was not over. McFadin had time to file a motion for new trial, and only after that was disposed of would McElroy's conviction become final. On June 30, McElroy swaggered into the D&G with a M-1 rifle and proceeded to describe, in detail, how he was going to shoot Bo and mutilate his body. Everyone knew that, under the terms of his bond, McElroy was not supposed to carry any firearms. The threats against Bo were too much for Pete Ward. He declared that he was going to provide an affidavit, stating that McElroy had violated his bond. Pete's two sons and another farmer, Gary Dowling, also signed affidavits. When McElroy found out, he confronted Ward and later stalked him with a gun. McElroy thought Del and Greg Clement provided affidavits, too (they hadn't), and he drove by their places to menace them.

The citizens of Skidmore were fed up with Ken McElroy. A group of them agreed to accompany Pete Ward and the others to McElroy's bond revocation hearing that was set for July 10. There, they hoped the judge would put McElroy in jail, pending the outcome of the posttrial motions. McFadin had another case set for July 10 and asked the prosecutor to agree to a continuance. He consented but only with the proviso that McFadin tell McElroy to stay away from Skidmore.

About sixty men gathered in Skidmore the morning of July 10 to go with Ward to the hearing. The crowd learned, to their astonishment, that McFadin had obtained yet another postponement, leaving McElroy on the street. Nodaway County sheriff Dan Estes showed up at the meeting. He told the frustrated crowd to form a neighborhood watch to keep an eye on McElroy's movements. Then, the sheriff left town. Not twenty minutes later, Ken and Trena McElroy showed up at the D&G. For once, he wasn't armed. The crowd found out that McElroy was in the tavern, and they trooped down there. The bar was full of angry citizens. Trena said, "Well, we'd better go." McElroy bought a six-pack of beer, and they left. Ken and Trena sat in his truck. Ken started to light a cigarette. A shot rang out, the back window of the truck shattered and Ken's head slumped down. A second shot rang out, and he slumped farther. Trena opened the passenger door, and a man pulled her out. She was covered with blood. She saw a man she identified as Del Clement with a rifle aimed at the truck. More shots, maybe ten in all, came from a .30-30 rifle, a .22 and a shotgun. Ken McElroy was dead.

McElroy's body laid in the truck for more than an hour before an ambulance arrived to take it away. Some of the townsfolk crept up to the cab to make sure he was, in fact, dead. Many were relieved. The police launched an investigation that quickly petered out. There were, perhaps, forty to sixty witnesses to the shooting, but no one aside from Trena named the shooters. One witness gave a name but recanted the next day. While no one threatened the witnesses, they provided the same kind of defense to his killers as McElroy used when he was the perpetrator—if no one was willing to testify, the shooters could not be tried. The refusal of anyone to come forward provided the trope that has dogged Skidmore ever since—a town that covered up the killing of the town "bully," although the word "bully" was hardly adequate to describe how McElroy terrorized anyone who incurred his wrath and tried to bring him to justice.

After the killing, Skidmore had to go through a different kind of ordeal—dealing with the media. The local and national press descended on the town. Its residents were often portrayed as rural hicks who finally took action, harkening back to nineteenth-century vigilantes. The big-name media came—*People* magazine, *Playboy* and even Morley Safer from *60 Minutes*.

When local law enforcement failed to charge a suspect, the FBI launched an investigation, and a federal grand jury was convened. None of the investigations went anywhere. No one except Trena would name the shooters.

Author Harry MacLean went to Skidmore to get the full story. He lived there for three years, pieced together the entire tale and published it in a best-selling book titled *In Broad Daylight*. MacLean emphasized that the people of Skidmore were peaceful, but their level of frustration with an ineffective legal system grew until it boiled over on July 10, 1981. He named the shooters as Del Clement and Gary Dowling and said there was possibly a third (unidentified) man who used a shotgun. Both Clement and Dowling consistently denied they were the shooters and are now dead. Neither was ever charged.

Ken McElroy was buried in St. Joseph. Trena offered a $5,000 reward to anyone who would come forward to testify. There was just one catch: they would have to wait to be paid from the film rights she and Gene McFadin were selling. Trena filed a wrongful death lawsuit against Clement, the town and the town's mayor. It was settled without any admission of liability (a typical provision) for $17,500. The murder case was never officially closed.

Skidmore might be the unluckiest town in America. One tragedy should be enough, but it had to go through two more. On April 11, 2001, Brandon Perry left his home in Skidmore to return a pair of jumper cables to a friend. He was never seen again. Brandon Perry's disappearance remains unsolved.

On December 16, 2004, Lisa Montgomery came to Skidmore to visit a very pregnant Bobbie Jo Stinnett, Brandon Perry's cousin, ostensibly to see about buying one of the rat terrier puppies she bred. Instead, she wanted Bobbie Jo's baby. Montgomery overpowered Bobbie Jo and cut the baby out of her womb. A witness to the scene later said it looked like Bobbie Jo's body had "exploded." Lisa took the baby back to her home in Melvern, Kansas. This time, there was no delay in the law enforcement response. The authorities tracked down Montgomery and arrested her the next day. The child was found unharmed.

In 2007, Montgomery was tried and convicted in federal court of kidnapping resulting in death. The jury recommended the death sentence, which the court duly imposed in 2008. Her conviction was affirmed in 2012. Lisa Montgomery was executed in January 2021; she was the first woman to be executed by the federal government since Bonnie Brown Heady.

13.

AMERICAN GOTHIC

In small-town papers across the country, there is often a column reporting the news of local residents, their families, their celebrations and their visitors. On January 7, 1987, the following news item appeared in the *Chillicothe* (Missouri) *Constitution Tribune*:

> *Wayne and Bonnie Copeland and children, Lester and Crystal, spent Christmas Eve with Wayne's parents, Mr. and Mrs. Ray Copeland, for a Christmas dinner and exchange of gifts. The Ray Copelands had Christmas telephone calls from their son, Sonny Copeland, in Phoenix, Ariz., and their daughter, Betty Gibson, in Louisville, Ky.*

Two years later, on October 9, 1989, Ray and Faye Copeland, an "elderly northwest Missouri couple," were arrested on charges of conspiracy to steal by using bad checks to purchase livestock. The big news wasn't the arrest but that their Mooresville farm was being "secretly" (in reality, not so secretly) searched by the sheriff of Livingston County. The sheriff refused to give details but "told reporters it should be clear what searchers are looking for," according to the *St. Joseph News-Press/Gazette*. And rumors flew that the search was for bodies. Nothing but "stuff" had been found so far, the sheriff said, but the search continued.

Ray Copeland was born in Oklahoma in 1914 (or 1915, the date is in dispute), one of five children. His parents were tenant farmers, and Ray only attended school until fourth grade. His older brother, John, in an interview with Michael McCann of the *St. Joseph News-Press/Gazette*, said Ray started his criminal activities at age eighteen, stealing from family members. He even stole from his parents, who, Ray's brother and sister claimed, spoiled him by giving him a pass on his bad actions. Others were not so forgiving. Ray was caught committing illegal activities ten times between 1938 and 1971; he was convicted and jailed six times for crimes including cattle theft, check forgery and writing bad checks.

Ray's wife, Faye, who ultimately became a coconspirator in his worst crimes, was only nineteen when she met the twenty-six-year-old Ray in 1940. At that time, he had already served his first six-month jail term. Faye was born in 1921 in Arkansas and was raised in a "good Christian home." She attended a one-room schoolhouse until eighth grade, when she left school to work and help support her family. Ray and Faye married after only six months and proceeded to have six children between 1941 and 1951. In addition to being a farm wife, Faye also worked as a laundress at the Chillicothe Glove Factory for eighteen years, and after that, she worked at an area motel, where she performed a variety of duties. She had to work, Faye said, to keep her children, who she essentially raised on her own, fed and clothed. The children said their father even stole from them. As soon as they were old enough to work, he encouraged them to open savings accounts for their earnings, and then he took those earnings from their accounts.

The Copeland family moved often, living in California, Illinois, Arkansas and Missouri. Ray served his second prison term for cattle theft in Arkansas in 1949. Faye and the children lived with Ray's brother John while he served his one-year term. In 1950, the Copeland family moved to Missouri for the first time. Ray was not long out of prison, and Faye was pregnant with their sixth child. When that child was two weeks old, Ray was arrested for stealing a calf from his employer. Although there is no record of his being convicted, Faye remembers her husband being sentenced to work on the judge's farm. For the next eleven years, the family lived in Illinois, moving abruptly and often. The Copelands' sons Al and Wayne figured their sudden moves were done so that their father could escape the law. He was, however, convicted of writing bad checks, usually to buy cattle, several times during their sojourn in Illinois, and he spent time incarcerated. During Ray's jail time, Faye had to work long hours and also collected welfare, even though Ray often spoke of how much he hated "welfare bums."

In 1966, the Copelands settled in Mooresville, Missouri, a small town a few miles from the bigger Chillicothe. They bought a house and a farm in 1967, and Ray hoped, but failed, to make their living farming. According to

Copeland, it wasn't his fault, but the fault of bankers and suppliers—anyone but him. Faye worked in a factory, and at times, Ray took on extra jobs, such as a position as a handyman. Among the news items of the family's visits, vacations, their son's army life and the births of grandchildren, a small wanted advertisement appeared in the Chillicothe paper in 1972, with Ray Copeland offering to do odd jobs. But mostly, Ray wanted to make money fast with the least amount of effort.

Ray thought he had come up with the perfect scheme when he decided that, instead of passing bogus checks himself, he would make himself a victim. He enlisted hitchhikers and transients he found at soup kitchens and homeless shelters and offered them better lives. Ray would teach them how to buy livestock and pay them $300 a week as they learned. Once engaged, the two men would attend a cattle auction, sitting apart but where they could see one another so Ray could signal when the partner should bid. The partner would pay with a bad check signed "Ray Copeland." Once the cattle were sold and the money was divided, the partner would leave town before the check failed to clear, and Ray would become a victim instead of a perpetrator.

Even though the police suspected Ray because of his history, he couldn't be prosecuted until he met Gerald Perkins. Perkins didn't follow the rules Ray had set out to make sure he could escape blame for the crimes. He stayed around long enough to be caught, and to save himself, he told the police about the scam. Ray was in his sixties by then, and although he was arrested, he couldn't be prosecuted because Perkins didn't stay around long enough to testify. The last time Faye bailed Ray out of jail for his participation in a cattle-buying scam, she gave him an ultimatum: "If you ever again get in any trouble of any sort, I will not help you. I will not even be around you because I don't believe in getting in trouble."

The ultimatum worked for sixteen years. Perhaps it took her husband that long to figure out the new, deadly twist to his cattle-buying scam. During this time, while Ray stayed out of trouble, Faye said that she began to trust him again. Things deteriorated when the family farm went into foreclosure. It was then that Ray began bringing home men who stayed for a short time and left quickly. While there, Faye said she cooked their meals and washed their clothes but didn't ask questions about what they were doing. When the bodies of the men who had worked for them were found near their farm, she said, "I don't think there was anybody more surprised than me." Ray's new plan was foolproof. His "partners" couldn't rat him out when Ray was finished with them because they were dead.

Even though Ray had added the protective layer of killing his partner after he had played his part in the scheme, Jack McCormick managed to escape before Ray could kill him. He called the Nebraska State Crime Stoppers in August 1989, after he had fled Missouri and the Copelands, to say he had found bones and a skull while at their farm. McCormick's new information took an inquiry into Copeland's cattle buying that began in 1986 to a new level. McCormick received $500 for the tip to the hotline.

On October 14, 1989, a major case squad entered the investigation at the Copeland farm to find "the whereabouts of people who had worked for them in the past." By October 16, the squad had found three bodies buried in shallow graves inside a barn at a farm where Ray Copeland had done work for the owner. The last renter to live at that farm said the barn had smelled bad, but he figured an animal had died inside the building. Forensic examination later concluded that the three victims had been killed execution style with one bullet from a shotgun to the back of the head. After the discovery of the three bodies, the search continued, concentrated on farms where Copeland had worked.

Rumors and talk about the search spread quickly around the small farming communities in the area. In interviews with reporters from the *St. Joseph News-Press/Gazette*, residents and neighbors described the couple as "loners who did not socialize and kept to themselves." They knew Ray had had trouble with the law, and some admitted they thought he "was not completely honest."

A fourth, badly decomposed body of a white male was discovered in a different barn in Livingston County on October 25. The body was found in a shallow grave under bales of hay—bales of hay that were placed in the barn by Ray Copeland. The identities of three of the victims were determined using dental records and a list of twenty names that had been found in the Copeland home of men who had been hired to work as farmhands by Ray Copeland from a homeless shelter in Springfield, Missouri. The victims were Paul Jason Cowart, twenty-one, of Dardanelle, Arkansas; John W. Freeman, twenty-seven, of Tulsa, Oklahoma; and Jimmie Dale Harvey, twenty-seven, of Springfield. The fourth body could not be identified right away. The men had all been incarcerated, and their dental records came from that source. Investigators also found a .22-caliber slug in the skull of one of the victims. It came from a weapon that was owned by Ray and Faye Copeland. Yet, they were still not charged with the murders.

Law enforcement used the list of names from the Copeland home as a starting point. Handwriting analysis showed that the list was written by Faye

Copeland. The names of the four men who were found buried were on the list, as were the names of some men who had been located alive. At the beginning of November 1989, eight of the men were still unaccounted for.

When the Copelands were arrested for conspiracy to steal, James Page was living with and working for the couple. He denied knowing anything about the livestock scam. He had been hired, he said, to listen to the auctioneers and transmit what they were saying to Ray Copeland, who claimed to not be able to hear. However, Copeland had opened both a checking account and a post office box for Page. This was one of the elements that led the police to look into bank activity of the transients who were hired by the Copelands. Evidence was mounting against the couple.

Finally, on November 13, 1989, both Ray and Faye Copeland were charged with three counts of first-degree murder, and the state gave notice that they would request the death penalty. When questioned as to whether the death penalty was necessary, given the age of the defendants, the attorney general answered that the death penalty had nothing to do with age but with the aggravating circumstances of the murders. A relative of one of the victims also filed a civil wrongful death suit against the Copelands, asking for monetary damages.

Even after the Copelands were charged with murder, the investigation continued, and a fifth body was found on November 22 in a well near the barn where the fourth body had been found. A Livingston County grand jury returned five indictments against the Copelands on December 27, 1989, resulting in additional charges being filed against the couple. The grand jury was called to bypass pretrial hearings. The two previously unidentified bodies were finally named as Dennis K. Murphy of Normal, Illinois, and Wayne Warner, whose address was unknown.

When the Copelands finally appeared in court on January 3, 1990, they pleaded not guilty to the five charges against them. Faye was "tearful" during her appearance, which was separate from that of her husband. The elderly couple was returned to jail after their appearances, this time, with bail revoked. A lot of legal wrangling continued between this court appearance and the trial. One of the main issues was where the trial should be held. Ray Copeland's attorneys argued that it would be impossible to have a fair trial in Livingston County because of all the surrounding publicity. The prosecution's position was that it would be prohibitively expensive to move the trial elsewhere, given the number of witnesses they planned to call. Meals, transportation and housing costs for the over two hundred witnesses would be enormous and borne by Livingston County. The final decision was to choose jurors for Ray's trial from Phelps County and bring them to Livingston County to hear the case. Meals and housing costs for the jurors were covered in any case because they were usually sequestered during such trials. Faye's jurors were imported from Vernon County.

While awaiting trial, Ray Copeland underwent back surgery and also "a complete neurological workup for senile dementia." The examination raised the question of whether Ray was competent to stand trial. Was he able to understand the proceedings against him, and did he possess the capability to assist in his defense?

The prosecution intended to try Ray first, but continued questions about his mental fitness delayed his trial. On October 29, 1990, the parties picked a jury of eight women and four men from Vernon County, and they were brought to Livingston County. Faye was then sixty-nine years old and facing the death penalty. Faye's lawyers relied on the contention that she was a passive, submissive and isolated farm wife who was also a victim. They claimed that she stayed out of her husband's business and had nothing to do with the murders of the five transients. Countering that, the prosecution wanted to show her as a coconspirator, as evidenced by the list of men's names, including those of the victims, in Faye's handwriting.

One of the key witnesses in the prosecution's case was Jack McCormick, the self-described alcoholic and tramp who had made the call that initiated the investigation. McCormick was, like the murder victims, hired from a Springfield homeless shelter for fifty dollars a day to help Ray Copeland buy cattle at auction. He recounted how he had first become uneasy with the Copelands when Ray had him open a post office box and a checking account in a nearby town. Ray told him the checking account was for him to use to buy cattle. His discomfort rose to fear on a morning when Faye had left the two of them alone at the farm. Ray asked him to help roust a raccoon from the barn and then stood behind him, holding a .22 rifle the entire time. When Copeland pulled a tractor and trailer into the barn, with a shovel and a roll of plastic in the trailer, he grew scared for his life. McCormick believed the only reason he wasn't killed that day was because he never took his eyes off Ray and the gun. McCormick said that, after the encounter in the barn, he insisted that Ray take him to the bank in Brookfield to withdraw money from the checking account. Ray agreed but first stopped in Chillicothe to talk to someone else. They encountered Faye, who, McCormick said, looked "real surprised" to see him. At the bank, he told the teller that he feared someone was trying to kill him. McCormick gave Ray the money he was due and parted company with the Copelands. He then drank himself into an alcoholic blackout.

He did report his fears and sighting of a human skull and bones on the Copelands' property to the Livingston County Sheriff's Office later that same day, but he didn't stay around to give an in-person report to the deputy who was sent to speak to him. After that, McCormick wandered through several western states before making a report to the Nebraska crime tip line and returning to Missouri. He admitted later that the report that stated he had seen a skull and human bones on the Copeland property was a lie. McCormick also denied that Faye was at all submissive and stated that she was very involved in her husband's affairs.

A neighbor of the Copelands, Bonnie Thompson, testified that she watched the farmer and his wife through binoculars; she said that Faye accompanied her husband on his trips to Springfield to recruit transients to assist in the cattle-buying scam. She also said that Ray spoke cruelly to Faye but said she had never seen him hit his wife or any bruises on Faye. Other witnesses testified that Faye often accompanied her husband on trips to the farms where the murdered transients were found.

Two other men who worked for the Copelands had similar experiences to that of Jack McCormick. They gave slightly different versions of Faye's involvement with her husband's business. One said Faye had gone to a cattle auction and viewed cattle with him. The other said that Faye was "reticent" and dominated by her husband. He also said that Ray gave him a fake name—Mr. Jones—when he hired him.

When bank officials were called to testify about the cattle-buying scheme, they all admitted Faye Copeland was never seen or named in any of their transactions with the murdered transients. But they did use bank statements to show that the dates of the last checks written by the victims to the cattle barns (and returned for insufficient funds) corresponded closely to the dates that forensic evidence determined the men were murdered on. The final prosecution witness testified about the infamous list of names written by Faye, which had an "X" beside the names of three of the victims. Faye sat silently, head down, throughout the entire parade of prosecution witnesses.

The first witnesses called by the defense were the Copelands' son and daughters-in-law, who told the jury what they observed about the relationship between Ray and Faye. They agreed that she was often verbally abused by her husband, who was described as "violent, uncommunicative, and illiterate." The son, Wayne Copeland, recounted that the couple argued about everything but said that his mom would not argue back; instead, she would up and leave. A daughter-in-law also testified that Faye kept the cattle-buying records for Ray, so she must have known about his activities.

A psychologist engaged by the defense was not allowed to testify in support of a battered-woman defense. The judge ruled that, under Missouri law, that defense was allowed only in cases claiming self-defense. Although it was a blow to their case, the defense attorneys still believed they could prevail.

After two and a half hours of deliberation, the jury returned a verdict of guilty on five counts of first-degree murder against Faye Copeland. Faye's response when the first guilty verdict was read was a simple: "Oh, no." By the time all five guilty verdicts had been returned, she had broken down in tears, saying, "I never done anything." Despite this assertion, the jury recommended four death sentences and one sentence of life imprisonment for the murders of five men who had been employed by Faye Copeland and her husband.

The arrest and subsequent incarceration of Faye Copeland in October 1989 were a first for her. And the initial charges were for writing bad checks. It wasn't until later, while Faye was still jailed, that the stakes were raised to the first-degree murder charges she was eventually convicted of. This broke her. In January 1991, after her conviction, Faye told *St. Joseph News-Press/Gazette* reporter Michael McCann, who covered the investigation and trial, "I just want to go home." She sobbed, "I just want to be myself again." While Faye was held in the Livingston County Jail, where she was the only woman prisoner, she called her sons, Al and Wayne, who lived on farms nearby, several times a day. And they visited her without fail every week. Her sons refused to believe their mother knew anything about what her husband had done. And how did Faye feel about the husband whose actions brought the law down on them? "I'll always love him but not as much now," she said. "He has done me great damage. I begged him time and time again to please stay out of trouble."

On the same day a recommendation of the death sentence was handed down for his wife, Faye, Ray Copeland's attorney offered a plea bargain to prosecutors: a plea of guilty if the death penalty was off the table. Prosecutors refused. Ray Copeland's defense team worked hard to have him declared incompetent to stand trial, and the prosecution worked equally hard to prove that he was competent. A defense neuropsychologist said that Ray was paranoid, delusional, psychotic and irrational, all of which made him unable to help his attorneys with his defense. The defendant believed there was a plot against him and his family involving "bankers, cattle barn operators, 'two colored guys and a white girl,' drifter Jack McCormick, and Livingston County prosecutor Doug Roberts." Experts for the prosecution said they found no evidence of delusions or paranoia.

Although Ray was diagnosed with "senile dementia," it was determined it did not prevent him from understanding what was happening to him at the trial. If he had been found mentally unfit, one of the outcomes could have been that Ray would have avoided a trial and been committed to the state hospital while his wife received the death penalty. At the end of the day, Ray Copeland was declared to be fit to stand trial. He, too, would face a jury and a possible death penalty.

Bill Smith, a reporter at the *St. Louis Post-Dispatch*, interviewed Ray Copeland while he was confined at the state psychiatric hospital in Fulton, Missouri, awaiting trial. This was Copeland's first interview since his arrest, and it was at his invitation that the reporter visited. "I never killed anybody in my life," he said. "Me and my wife lived together for fifty years. We never killed nobody; we never hurt nobody, and we never talked about hurting nobody." At times during the interview, in which he constantly denied committing the murders, he cried, especially when he spoke of his wife. Ray explained that he had hired the transients to help him at cattle auctions because he couldn't hear, and he said that every one of the men had stolen money from him. He also reminded the reporter that he had given law enforcement the hint of where to find the body in the well. Why would he have done that if he had put the body there?

At the eleventh hour, Ray Copeland's defense attorneys worked out a plea deal with Livingston County prosecutor Doug Roberts. In exchange for Ray voluntarily pleading guilty to killing the five men, the death penalty would be taken off the table. The deal also involved taking the death penalty off the table for Faye Copeland. Roberts supported the deal, but state assistant attorney general Kenneth Hulshof, who was helping prosecute the case, did not. Hulshof believed that the commission of such callous crimes warranted the death penalty, regardless of the age of the defendant or the cost of the trial. When the presiding judge rejected the plea deal, he also removed Prosecutor Roberts from the case, citing conflict of interest because he had, at one time, represented the Copelands in a civil case. This reversed the judge's earlier ruling, when the defense team's motion to remove the prosecutor for the same reason was denied. The defense's response was to request the judge be removed and replaced. The court of appeals refused the request, and Judge E. Richard Webber remained on the case.

The parties attempted to choose a jury from Phelps County, but after three days, it became clear that it would be impossible to pick an unbiased jury from that county because too many people had heard about the case and had opinions about it. The judge ordered the jury selection be moved to St. Louis County, where it commenced—again—on February 19, 1991. Once chosen, the jury was transported to Livingston County for the trial.

The long-awaited trial of Ray Copeland for murder of five men he hired as farmhands to assist him in buying cattle finally began on March 7. The defense attorneys did not seriously contest his guilt; rather, their strategy was to prove that Ray was senile and should be committed to a state mental hospital rather than sentenced to death row. The prosecution once again laid out the case that Ray had committed the murders in the course of a planned cattle-buying scheme in which he and his wife had made a profit of $32,000; this closely followed the evidence that was presented against Faye. One difference was the number of the victims' family members who testified, tying Ray to their sons and grandsons by identifying clothing or saying they saw Ray with the victim. After a defense of only five rebuttal witnesses, the case was given to the jury. On Monday, March 18, in front of a packed courtroom, they handed down guilty verdicts for all five counts of first-degree murder.

In the sentencing phase of Ray's trial, the defense called experts to support the claim that he should be spared the death penalty because he was senile. Ray sat impassively as the jury recommended a death sentence for his crimes. Others in the courtroom were more emotional. Some jurors fought tears, and even the prosecutor admitted that anytime a person is sentenced to death, there are mixed emotions. As defense attorneys tried to comfort Copeland, he only said, "It's okay."

The Copelands' household items and farm implements were sold at auction soon after the end of the trials. People were there, looking not only for bargains, but for souvenirs of the murders. Several shovels and spades sold for $21 apiece and were thought to have perhaps been used to dig the shallow graves of the victims. The proceeds totaled $7,500.

Faye Copeland was sentenced to death by lethal injection by Judge Richard Webber on April 27, 1991, following the recommendation of the jury. She visibly winced at the pronouncement and then proclaimed her innocence. Her sons, Al and Wayne, continued to believe their mother was innocent. Her attorney said Faye, too, was a victim of Ray Copeland. Faye Copeland was the only woman on Missouri's death row.

Ray Copeland, who was convicted of committing the most "heinous and horrendous" serial murders ever in the state of Missouri, joined his wife on death row after being sentenced by Judge Webber to death by lethal injection for those murders. Copeland, seventy-six, was the oldest person on death row in the country, and his wife, sixty-nine, was the oldest woman.

They were also the only married couple to be so sentenced. By the time Ray Copeland died—not by lethal injection, but due to a stroke in October 1993—he and Faye were no longer the only married couple on death row. Zeih and Maria Isa, who were convicted of the murder of their daughter, had also been sentenced to death.

Faye Copeland received a birthday gift on her seventy-eighth birthday. Her death sentence was commuted to life imprisonment. She, too, escaped the death penalty when she died of natural causes on December 28, 2003. Faye had suffered a stroke in August 2002 and had been medically paroled to a nursing home before her death. In 1999, still professing her innocence of the heinous murders of which she'd been convicted, she admitted that marrying Ray Copeland had been the "worst mistake of [her] life."

14.

THE MISSOURI MIRACLE

Not many crime stories have an ending that offers much hope, but the kidnapping of Shawn Hornbeck is a different story. Often called the Missouri Miracle, Shawn's rescue resulted not only in his return, but in the return of a second boy as well. Here's to happy endings!

It was the kind of Sunday in October that kids live for—sunny and warm, with no sign of the coming cold. Shawn Damien Hornbeck had left home around 1:00 p.m. on his lime green bicycle, heading for a nearby friend's home. When he wasn't home as it started to grow dark around 6:00 p.m., his mother, Pam Akers, set out to check on him. He had never arrived at the friend's house. Pam's worry grew. Her son was afraid of the dark and never stayed away from home once night fell. She called police. This was not normal behavior for her son. The only reported sighting of Shawn that afternoon was by a sheriff's deputy who was answering an alarm at a local business. He saw Shawn riding his bicycle along a nearby road around 4:30 p.m., but after that, the boy seemingly vanished.

Searchers, numbering in the hundreds, came from all over. As temperatures fell, they spent Sunday night and all day Monday searching for Shawn within a two-mile radius of his home—eventually expanded to a wider area. The terrain around Richwoods, Missouri, where Shawn lived with his mother and stepfather, Craig Akers, is a former mining area dotted with woods, sinkholes, lakes, ponds and mine shafts. Volunteers rode ATVs and horses and searched on foot and even by helicopter—but to no avail. The FBI was also brought in to help with the search.

Shawn was eleven years old, about four feet eight inches tall and weighed ninety pounds when he disappeared. He attended fifth grade at Richwoods School. On the day he went missing, he was wearing jeans and an orange Astros T-shirt, his little-league team. The boy liked video games, SpongeBob and wanted to work with computers, like his stepdad, when he grew up. Theories quickly grew around his disappearance. He'd fallen off his bike and was too injured to make it home, he'd been hit by a car, encountered foul play or, when no sign of him was found, it was predicted that he was abducted.

By Tuesday, there were two searches—law enforcement and search and rescue—in progress. The teams were cooperating and sharing information. Law enforcement declared the disappearance a criminal matter at that point. The lead FBI agent said it was a "situation where a young boy [had] disappeared without a trace." He continued, "No sightings have been had, no evidence has been found. The search and rescue effort will continue in earnest." The second team of people from the area stated that, until there was evidence that the boy was *not* in the area, the search would continue. Shawn was a healthy boy, one of the volunteers said, and could go several days without food and water. The dropping temperatures, however, caused concern. One of the puzzles was that, along with no sign of Shawn, there was no sign of his bicycle; it was a lime green color that should have been easy to spot.

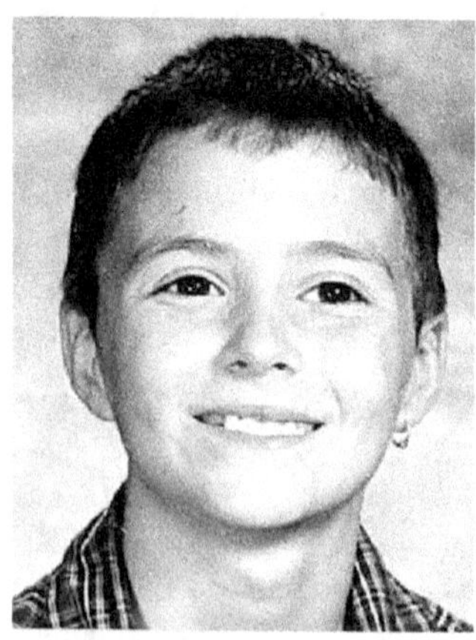

This photograph of Shawn Hornbeck was widely distributed when he disappeared. It even appeared on national missing children flyers. *Courtesy of the* Daily Journal *(Flat River, Missouri).*

Family members appeared on television, asking for information about Shawn. It was front-page news in papers across the state, but there was still nothing. A member of the family said they were starting to believe Shawn had been abducted. There was no other explanation.

On Wednesday evening, following Shawn's Sunday disappearance, the official search was scaled back. The law enforcement search was operating out of the fire department. This was a hard decision, the fire chief in charge said, but they would be available to help with any specific leads that came in. However, family and friends declared they would continue on their own, operating from a local church. "We are not going to stop. We will stop when we find him," said Shawn's stepfather. Volunteers pinned yellow ribbons with Shawn's initials on their coats. A tip line was also set up for people to call in with any information they had regarding Shawn's disappearance, as well as a website.

A week later, there were still no leads on Shawn's disappearance. His father was still wearing the same hand-painted T-shirt he'd been wearing the day his son disappeared. He washed it at night and vowed to wear it every day until Shawn returned. Craig Akers was Shawn's stepfather, but he joined the family when Shawn was barely a year old and was the only father the boy had ever known. Shawn's biological father was dead. Family members are often investigated in cases of child disappearance, but law enforcement was quick to assure the public that the family was in no way connected with Shawn's disappearance.

On October 17, law enforcement closed its command center in Richwoods, and the agents and officers returned to their respective offices to continue the inquiry. The task force failed to turn up any clues or information regarding the disappearance. The volunteer search effort continued, with dwindling numbers of volunteers turning out. The family pleaded for more help to find their son. A staff member from the National Center for Missing and Exploited Children offered the family encouragement: "In cases similar to Shawn's, 60 percent of the children are recovered alive." He noted that children are sometimes found months or years after being abducted and that Shawn's case was still "fresh."

At the end of October, the tip line was receiving five to nine tips per day. National TV exposure on *Without a Trace* and *America's Most Wanted* was in the works. On Halloween, people gave out flyers with information about Shawn's disappearance along with candy. The reward fund was growing, and yet, there was not one concrete bit of information on where Shawn might have been.

The family grew frustrated with the Washington County Sheriff's Office, as days passed with seemingly nothing happening on Shawn's case. Finally, on November 12, they picketed the office, asking for more frequent updates and for the sheriff to call in the Major Case Squad. The squad is a force of local law enforcement that investigates serious cases in the area. The sheriff, Gary Yount, assured the family that leads were being followed and said that it was too late for the Major Case Squad.

Law enforcement, including the Missouri Highway Patrol, FBI and the Washington County Sheriff's Department, had put 2,290 hours of investigation into Shawn's disappearance as of November 22, 2002. They followed up on 319 leads and interviewed over 100 people. Two criminal investigators from the Missouri Highway Patrol's division of Drug and Crime Control and one FBI agent worked practically full-time on the case. Two local investigators worked on nothing but Shawn's case. In addition, 1,269 volunteers had logged over 16,500 hours, expanding the search over seven counties. And still, nothing.

Leads drifted in and were religiously checked, but rumors were also abundant. One of the stories that appeared again and again was that Shawn was hit by a car, taken to another location and murdered. Another story was that Shawn had come across a hidden meth lab and was killed to prevent him from telling. At times, it was difficult to sort out rumors from true leads—if any of the stories were true leads.

One of the problems in a missing person case if the person is not found right away is that attention drifts away. Other things happen—good and bad—and refocus the news spotlight. The Akerses, in their ceaseless search for Shawn, figured out a way to keep that from happening and to help others at the same time. They formed the nonprofit Shawn Hornbeck Foundation to share what they had learned during their search to help other families with missing children. This meant every time a child went missing, they stepped in with search-and-rescue help, visited the family and attended festivals to pass out information on keeping children safe. At the same time, they would mention their son and remind the public that he was still missing.

As Christmas approached in 2002, the Akers family, of course, had only one wish: for Shawn to return home. They said he would be delighted with the pile of gifts awaiting him, many from people he didn't even know. The one activity they planned for Christmas Day was to follow Shawn's known route from October 6, a route they had traveled many times—each time, hoping for some shred of evidence leading to Shawn.

In January 2003, Shawn's photograph and information appeared in a flyer that was mailed to millions of homes across the country by a company called ADVO. ADVO created its America's Looking for Its Missing Children campaign in 1985. One out of every seven children featured on the flyers was recovered safely. While the information went national, search operations continued in Washington County, where Shawn had disappeared.

Under the banner of the Shawn Hornbeck Foundation, Pam and Craig Akers started a program to make sure parents had the necessary information available to help in the search for their children in the event they went missing. A disk with their child's digital fingerprints, a current photograph and a form to fill out with their child's vital statistics was provided by the foundation. The information could be easily formatted and used to print flyers. It was yet another way to keep Shawn front and center as they continued to seek information about where he might be.

Whenever a missing child was found—such as the return of Elizabeth Smart from Utah after nine months—it gave the Hornbeck family a reason to smile. There was hope their son might still be alive and returned safely, despite the passage of time. Plus, Shawn's information was broadcast again, keeping his name out there to remind people he was still missing.

Six months after Shawn went missing, with no progress in the case, the reward for the boy's safe return reached $75,000. "You have stolen the past 194 days of our lives and forced us to live with the indescribable agony of not knowing where our son is," said his mother in a news article that announced the reward increase in the *Flat River Daily Journal*. She renewed her call for information on her boy. Birthdays came and went. Holidays were celebrated in Shawn's absence, but he remained missing without a trace.

That was, until Ben Ownby of Beaufort, Missouri, in Franklin County, Missouri, disappeared after the school bus dropped him off on January 8, 2007. Ben was thirteen years old, about four feet ten inches tall and weighed 105 pounds. He was a Boy Scout, loved computer games and was a good student. He was wearing a Rams windbreaker, jeans and tennis shoes when he disappeared. The only information available was given by a classmate, Mitchell Hults, who saw a white pickup with a camper shell and black Nissan lettering across the tailgate speed away at the time Ben went missing. And that white Nissan pickup truck would prove to be the undoing of the kidnapper.

Kirkwood, Missouri police spotted the Nissan in an apartment parking lot when they were serving an unrelated warrant. When the owner, Michael Devlin, appeared outside, the officers questioned him. They felt uneasy about the man when he refused to permit them entry into his apartment, and they contacted the FBI. Later, police said they also spoke with Shawn, who identified himself as "Shawn Wilcox," Devlin's godson. They did not recognize him as the boy who had been missing for four years. They were focused on finding Ben Ownby. After being notified by the Kirkwood police, the FBI put Devlin under surveillance and arrested him at his place of work, Imo's Pizza in Kirkwood, the next morning. They then rescued not only Ben Ownby, who had disappeared earlier in the week, but Shawn Hornbeck, who had disappeared over four years earlier.

Kirkwood is an affluent, tree-lined suburb of twenty-seven thousand people located in St. Louis County, Missouri. It has a downtown, a city hall and a small-town feel. People know one another, and in discussing the case, they remarked that finding two kidnapped boys was a very "un-Kirkwood-like" thing. Shawn's photograph was displayed on a bench at a nearby grocery store that was only blocks from where he'd lived. People throughout the community wondered if Shawn had ridden or walked right past them and they hadn't put the puzzle together. How could the boy have been hidden in plain sight in this community for so long?

When law enforcement officials suspected that Ben Ownby was in the apartment along with a teenage boy, one of the officers mused, "Wouldn't it be unbelievable if that was Shawn Hornbeck?" The boys were rescued on Friday afternoon, and after being checked by a physician at a local hospital, they were reunited with their very happy parents.

Who was the man who kidnapped the two boys? He was forty-one years old and worked at a nearby pizza parlor, part of a local chain, that was located close to the Kirkwood Police Station. He grew up in nearby Webster Groves and graduated from Webster Groves High School. He had a part-time job answering phones overnight at a local funeral home. Michael Devlin was adopted as an infant by a family with three adopted brothers and two sisters who were his parents' biological children. The family was comfortably well-off. Since he was overweight as he grew up, Devlin, nicknamed "Devo," was teased and became somewhat of a loner. He went to work at Imo's while he was still in high school, and that's where he stayed. His boss said he was a good worker and never caused trouble. He developed diabetes and had to have toes amputated as a complication of the disease. The thing everyone said about him after learning he had kidnapped two boys was that they never had the slightest reason to suspect him of anything of the kind. Devlin was never a suspect until he was.

Both the Ownby and the Akers families were hounded by news media after the boys were rescued. The families made appearances on national television shows, including the *Today* show, *Dateline* and *The Oprah Winfrey Show*. In a taped interview with Oprah, Shawn said that, every day, he prayed his family would find him, and he said he had low moments when he almost gave up hope, but he knew his parents wouldn't give up on him. He said, "I felt their hope and love."

Shawn seemed to be hidden in plain sight the entire time he was missing. He even had two encounters with police. He was stopped in 2006 while riding his bicycle late at night because, the officer said, he was wearing dark clothing and had no reflector on his bicycle. He gave his name as Shawn Devlin and was sent on his way with a warning. He also had a bike stolen in 2003 and reported it to the police under the name Shawn Devlin. It was not the green mountain bike he was riding when he was abducted. Neighbors knew the young man lived with Devlin and assumed he was Devlin's son. Shawn had friends he socialized with, a cellphone, internet access and a girlfriend he attended dances with. He went to the mall and had a bike he was free to ride around town. He also posted on the Shawn Hornbeck Foundation website. In December 2005, under the name Shawn Devlin, he asked how long the family was planning to look for their son. He also offered to write a poem for the family in a second post. When interviewed by Oprah Winfrey, he said he posted to give some kind of a hint.

But why didn't he tell anyone he was being held against his will? He was afraid. Devlin threatened to kill Shawn and his entire family, and he used a handgun to enforce that fear. Law enforcement recovered three guns at the apartment. Shawn was so traumatized by what had happened to him, especially early in the abduction, that he had come to see Devlin as a surrogate parent. He even watched Ben after he was brought into the house so Devlin could go to work.

Charges piled up against Michael Devlin as law enforcement interviewed the boys. Interviews proceeded slowly, giving the boys space to come to terms with all that was happening. Devlin faced charges in both Washington County, where Shawn was abducted, and Franklin County, where he took Ben. His bail was increased to $3 million. He was also investigated for his connection with other missing children, but nothing was found. What worried him about his arrest? "I don't know how I'm going to explain myself to my parents."

Shawn was showered with gifts from well-wishers on his return to his family. But the biggest gift the family was given was a new home. A local building company and its employees announced they would build the family a new four-bedroom house on their existing property, and it was to include an office space for the Shawn Hornbeck Foundation.

The Richwood School District engaged tutors to help Shawn catch up on his schoolwork. He had not attended school during his abduction. By May, Shawn was beginning to go out to local events, always accompanied by a family member. It was difficult, his parents said, to keep the media away from their son. As much as they appreciated all the help the media gave them while Shawn was missing, they were ready to step out of the spotlight. The Shawn Hornbeck Foundation was still up and running, and the Akerses spent as much as thirty hours a week working there in addition to their regular jobs. Their hope was that, someday, Shawn would take over the foundation and work with children to teach them how to stay safe.

Shawn spent his sixteenth birthday, his first after his rescue, raising money for the Shawn Hornbeck Foundation at a celebrity golf tournament in Madison, Illinois. This event also marked the first time Shawn was present at an event with a media presence. The media was not allowed to talk to him. Shawn's stepdad, Craig Akers, said Shawn wanted to help with the foundation and that he was ready to go back to school. He said Shawn would attend an unidentified private school in the fall.

The young people who were Shawn's friends while he was a captive of Michael Devlin missed him, and they wondered if their friendships didn't help him through his ordeal. Some of the friends lived nearby, while others only knew Shawn virtually. All of them hoped to reconnect someday, if not soon. Mental health professionals said that, although the friendships were valuable at the time, they would remind Shawn of his captivity and become a block to his healing process.

Michael Devlin faced charges not only in Washington and Franklin Counties, but also in St. Louis County and federal court. He agreed to plead guilty, relieving the courts of the burden of a trial, but it mostly kept the boys, Shawn and Ben, from having to give evidence. This resulted in multiple life sentences for the kidnapper. Devlin was at peace with his decision. He had his attorney deliver the message that he wanted to spare his family and Shawn Hornbeck the anguish of a trial. When he finally appeared in court, he admitted that he had kidnapped, sexually assaulted and tried to kill Shawn Hornbeck. He also admitted to kidnapping and sexually assaulting Ben Ownby. But Devlin did not offer one word of apology to the victims (who were not present in court). Michael Devlin was sentenced to spend the rest of his life in prison.

After Devlin pleaded guilty, the details he recounted in the courtroom came out in the media. He told of how he first spotted Shawn on his bicycle and watched him. When Shawn turned down a gravel road, Devlin followed and bumped the bicycle with his vehicle. He got out of his truck and feigned concern, then forced Shawn into the truck and duct taped his hands. He told the boy "he was in the wrong place at the wrong time." When they returned to Devlin's apartment, he tied Shawn to a futon and duct taped his mouth. He did this for the first thirty days of his captivity, returning home during his work breaks to feed the boy and let him go to the bathroom. At night, he would tie Shawn to his wrist or his waist before they went to sleep. He also continually assaulted him. After about thirty days, he drove Shawn to the country and started to choke him, but Shawn talked him out of it by telling Devlin he would forget about his attempt to kill him and be glad to be alive. He also said he didn't have to worry about leaving him at the apartment alone. Devlin decided to take another boy because "Shawn was getting too old." And he made Shawn help him with that abduction, both angering the boy and making him fearful. Why would Devlin keep him around if he had a new boy?

Despite all they had been through, the boys, their parents reported, were doing well. Ben returned to school two weeks after his ordeal, and his parents kept him out of the spotlight. Shawn attended a private school and was making good grades. His parents said that they were seeing more of the boy then than they had before he disappeared. Shawn gave an interview to the *St. Louis Post-Dispatch* in 2013, when three women were rescued from long-term captivity in Cleveland, Ohio. He was twenty-one years old at the time and was working full time at a metal fabricating company. He said he liked working with his hands. Sporting two tattoos—"Faith" on one forearm and "Respect" on the other—he said, "you need 'em both." He was still living with his parents and knew he'd always be known as "the kidnapped boy from Richwoods."

In June 2014, the Shawn Hornbeck Foundation, which was created by Pam and Craig Akers while their son was missing, ceased operation. Shawn has remained out of the spotlight since then.

15.

ONE MINUTE AND THIRTY-TWO SECONDS

The Kirkwood City Hall Shooting

One minute and thirty-two seconds is all it took for Charles "Cookie" Thornton to shoot and kill five people inside the city council chamber in Kirkwood, Missouri, and wound two others. He had already killed one police officer on his way to the meeting. Thornton parked his converted hearse, met Kirkwood police sergeant William Biggs on a parking lot across from city hall and shot him. Thornton took Biggs's gun and headed to city hall. As Biggs lay wounded and dying, he managed to send a distress signal.

The group at city hall had just finished the Pledge of Allegiance when Thornton, carrying a protest sign, burst into the chamber and shouted, "Everybody stop what you're doing! Hands in the air!" He opened fire, first killing police officer Thomas Ballman, then targeting public works director Ken Yost and killing him. He moved to the front of the room and shot and killed council members Connie Karr and Michael H.T. Lynch before critically wounding Mayor Michael Swoboda. Council members Tim Griffin, Iggy Yuan and Art McDonnell were also sitting on the dais and escaped. He also wounded Todd Smith, a *Suburban Journals* reporter. Next, he targeted city attorney John Hessel, who ran to the back of the room and threw chairs at him, warding off the attack long enough for additional police officers to arrive and shoot Thornton, ending the spree with his death.

What happened to incite such a violent reaction in a man who so many people said was the life of the party, someone who always wore a big smile and who was known as an "uncle" by many children he mentored in his Meacham Park neighborhood? Thornton would say he had his reasons.

A front view of Kirkwood City Hall, the site of the City Hall Massacre. *Photograph by the author.*

For several years, he had been a city hall fixture, protesting his treatment by Kirkwood officials. He blamed his troubles on the fact that he was a Black man in a predominantly white community, and for that reason, he was receiving unfair treatment. Much of his anger was directed toward the city council and the mayor, in particular. Thornton accused the council of lying, discriminating against him and exploiting the majority Black neighborhood where he lived, Meacham Park, for white profit. He had been arrested twice at council meetings for disorderly conduct. He ultimately sued the city to be allowed his free speech at meetings, but a federal judge rejected his argument on January 28, 2008, only days before the shooting.

Cookie Thornton, called "Cookie" because that was his first word, had grown up in Meacham Park. He had graduated from Kirkwood High School, where he was a track star and set state records. Thornton attended church regularly, and instead of saying "hello" and "goodbye," he bestowed blessings. He graduated from Northeast Missouri State University (now Truman State University) and set up an asphalt and demolition business. He regularly parked his equipment on his parents' residential property in Meacham Park.

Meacham Park, Thornton's home, was, for many years, an unincorporated Black community lying between Big Bend Road and I-44. It was a close-knit community with churches, a school and neighbors people could rely upon.

But like many areas, it fell victim to urban decay with all its problems—no jobs but plenty of drugs and crime—and no way to make St. Louis County take notice and do something about it. Meacham Park was annexed by Kirkwood in 1991. Thornton was in favor of the annexation, looking at it as an opportunity to improve his community.

However, things did not work out as planned. Because Thornton had parked his vehicles on private property for over twenty years, he figured he was grandfathered in, but Kirkwood officials quickly disabused him of that notion, and he was cited for parking his vehicles illegally. For a while, he rented property and parked his equipment there until the cost became too expensive. Thornton had spent money on new equipment and was expecting to win a contract with the city to build Kirkwood Commons.

Kirkwood Commons was one of the reasons the city was anxious to annex Meacham Park. A portion of that neighborhood was prime retail real estate, as it was bordered by three major roads: Big Bend, Kirkwood Road and I-44. It was perfect for development as a shopping center with big-box stores, like Target, Walmart and Lowe's. After annexation, the city took two-thirds of Meacham Park to make room for the shopping center. A large portion of the land taken had been Section 8 housing that had been built by St. Louis County. They promoted the venture to Meacham Park residents, saying money from the project would be used to improve the rest of the neighborhood and that the shopping center would provide jobs. By choosing the Meacham Park location, it also avoided the furor that such a development would cause elsewhere in the city. Plus, Kirkwood would receive sales tax revenue from the increased retail business.

Included in the agreement was a clause requiring the developer to use minority-owned businesses for portions of the work. The mayor of Kirkwood at that time, Marge Schramm, said that clause included all minority-owned businesses and not just the one owned by Thornton. But Thornton may have misunderstood. This disappointment only added to his disillusionment with Kirkwood city officials.

In 1999, Thornton filed for bankruptcy and resumed parking his equipment illegally. He was ticketed repeatedly. Thornton said Kirkwood was making it impossible for him to earn a living. He started showing up at city council meetings, saying that the city was involved in a "racist conspiracy" and had a "plantation mentality." Thornton was ticketed nineteen times in 2001, amassing $12,250 in fines. In 2002, he was fined an additional $6,200 for twenty-six tickets. The city finally stopped issuing violations when he'd amassed one hundred tickets and $20,000 in fines.

City attorney John Hessel offered Thornton a deal in 2002. If Cookie would follow the law going forward—stop parking in residential areas and stop throwing trash on vacant lots—the city would forgive his $20,000 in fines. Thornton wouldn't agree. He wanted the city to admit they had treated him wrongly.

Franklin McCallie, the former principal of Kirkwood High School and a civil rights activist, witnessed Cookie Thornton's behavior at a city council meeting in 2003. When he discovered the behavior had been going on for years, he stepped in and offered to help find a solution. By this time, Thornton was braying and he-hawing at meetings, laying in the aisle when he wasn't recognized to speak and picketing the city attorney's office and home, as well as the mayor's home. McCallie examined Thornton's tickets and found only one mistake. Instead of following McCallie's advice and taking the settlement, Thornton immediately used that one mistake as ammunition to charge racism. After four months, McCallie stepped back. He later wished he'd looked further into what was fueling Thornton's outrage.

Hessel offered another deal in 2003, but Thornton insisted that the city admit it was wrong. The lawyer told him to go ahead and sue. Thornton did and lost—then he appealed and lost. His demands grew. Thornton wanted a public apology and $25 million. Despite his mounting debt, he filed a federal lawsuit, mortgaging his parents' home to finance it. He also started dropping out of his community activities, focusing only on his case against Kirkwood. But still, no one believed this would end in violence.

Racial tensions in Kirkwood were mounting during this time. In 2005, Sergeant Bill McEntee, a Kirkwood police officer, was shot and killed by a Meacham Park resident who believed the police were responsible for his brother's death. The shooter's brother came home, collapsed and died after telling his grandmother that the police had been chasing him to find out where that brother was. The child had a congenital heart defect. Later that evening, McEntee answered a fireworks complaint call in Meacham Park and was killed.

Over 70 percent of the residents in both Kirkwood and Meacham Park voted for annexation. At the time, Meacham Park needed services that the county, which was then responsible for the area, either didn't or wouldn't provide. Kirkwood, in the process of building Kirkwood Commons, tore down old Section 8 housing that had been put up by the county to build new houses, fix up streets and enforce stricter laws. Some residents missed the old, relaxed ways of the county. Residents wanted Meacham Park to remain residential even after annexation, but two-thirds of it disappeared into commercial development. Kirkwood put money into new housing, but few

Above: The City of Kirkwood created a monument to those who were killed February 7, 2008. Today, it is a lovely shaded walk alongside the city hall. *Photograph by the author.*

Left: The walk commemorating the lives of the victims of the City Hall Massacre. Each light illuminates a stone that bears the name of one of the victims. *Photograph by the author.*

residents took advantage of the offer. This neighborhood was Thornton's home and a place he had worked all his life to make a better place.

Another point of contention in Meacham Park was how to use the old Turner School building. The building was where Meacham Park residents had attended school until it was closed and children were bused to various Kirkwood schools. It was a beautiful building that meant something to the residents, and they wanted it turned into a community center, a place where the kids in the neighborhood could go. Kirkwood turned down the proposal because it was too expensive, and it said there was already a community center only a mile and a half away. The building was turned into an office building, and Kirkwood gave the area a park instead—a park that closed at sundown.

How much did the divide between Meacham Park and Kirkwood contribute to Thornton's outrage and resulting behavior? It was the annexation and his spending on his business, followed by the failure to be given the work he thought he was promised, that started his disillusionment. And that disillusionment grew as time passed.

One of his victims was Connie Karr. She was a wife and mother serving her second term on the council, and she was a candidate for mayor. She had also worked hard as secretary of the Meacham Park Neighborhood Improvement Association. She wanted Meacham Park to have representation on the council, and she wanted to resolve the council's problems with Thornton. She was the fourth person and first council member shot. Michael Lynch had been on the council since 2000. He was the fifth person killed. Mayor Michael Swoboda did not die from his wounds initially, but he eventually succumbed to complications from a head wound on September 6, 2008. He had been mayor since 2000 and was finishing up his term of office. He had been very active in city and regional affairs for many years. Ken Yost was public works director and had also served as city engineer. He had a longtime contentious relationship with Thornton. Thomas Ballman had been a Kirkwood police officer since 1999. He was an active volunteer in the city and worked with youth organizations. William Biggs was the first to be killed and the last to be buried. He had been a police officer in Kirkwood for more than twenty years, and his sending of a distress call after he was shot was seen as a heroic effort that saved lives. The city built a memorial path to the victims next to city hall.

The first city council meeting in the reopened chambers occurred on March 6, 2008. A standing-room-only crowd, predominantly white, filled the room. The only Black people in attendance sat in a group in the back row of chairs. Police officers stood in the four corners of the chamber.

BIBLIOGRAPHY

Atchison (KS) *Champion.*

Boggs, Johnny D. *Jesse James and the Movies.* Jefferson, NC: McFarland & Company Inc., 2011.

Brennan, Ellen M. Email to the Audrain County Historical Society. November 26, 2010.

Brown, Buster. "History of Washington, MO." www.washingtonmo.com.

Brown, Cecil. *Stagolee Shot Billy.* Cambridge, MA: Harvard University Press, 2003.

———. "We Done Them Wrong: The Ballad of Frankie and Johnny." In *The Rose and the Briar: Death, Love and Liberty in the American Ballad.* Greil Marcus and Sean Wilentz, eds. New York: W.W. Norton & Company, 2005, 123–45.

Bus Stop Reads. "Bertha Gifford: The Angel of Death." www.goldmineguides.com. January 2015.

Chillicothe (MO) *Constitution Tribune.*

Clavin, Tom. *Wild Bill: The True Story of the American Frontier's First Gunfighter.* New York: St. Martin's Press, 2019.

Daily Journal (Flat River, MO).

Daily News (New York).

Dreiser, Theodore. *A History of Myself: Newspaper Days.* New York: Horace Liveright Inc., 1931.

Erwin, Vicki Berger. *Images of America: Mexico.* Charleston, SC: Arcadia Publishing, 2010.

Fanning, Diane. *Baby Be Mine: The Shocking True Story of a Woman Accused of Murdering a Pregnant Mother to Steal Her Child*. New York: St. Martin's Paperbacks, 2006.

Fowler, Giles. *Deaths on Pleasant Street: The Ghastly Enigma of Colonel Swope and Doctor Hyde*. Kirksville, MO: Truman State University Press, 2009.

Gardner, Mark Lee. *Shot All to Hell: Jesse James, the Northfield Raid, and the Wild West's Greatest Escape*. New York: William Morrow, 2013.

Genealogy Trails. "Franklin, MO." www.genealogytrails.com.

Guggenheim, Charles E. "Internet Movie Database." www.imdb.com.

Heidenry, John. *Zero at the Bone: The Playboy, the Prostitute, and the Murder of Bobby Greenlease*. New York: St. Martin's Press, 2009.

Internet Broadway Database. "McQueen, Steve." www.ibdb.com.

Internet Movie Database. "McQueen, Steve." www.imdb.com.

Kansas City Star.

King, Jeffrey S. *The Life and Death of Pretty Boy Floyd*. Kent, OH: Kent State University Press, 1998.

Krajicek, David J. *True Crime Missouri*. Mechanicsburg, PA: Stackpole Books, 2011.

Linder, Douglas O. "Famous Trials: Celia, a Slave, Trial." www.famous-trials.com.

Louisville Daily Journal.

MacLean, Harry N. *In Broad Daylight*. Seattle, WA: CreateSpace, 2016.

McLaurin, Melton A. *Celia, a Slave*. Athens: University of Georgia Press, 1991.

Meigs, William M. *The Life of Thomas Hart Benton*. Philadelphia, PA: J.P. Lippincott, 1904.

Mexico Intelligencer.

Mexico Ledger.

Murphy, S. Kay. *The Tainted Legacy of Bertha Gifford*. Seattle, WA: CreateSpace, 2016.

Newsom, Celia v. State of Missouri. Missouri Supreme Court (1855). Box 356, File 14, www.s1.sos.mo.gov.

Nichols, George W. "Wild Bill." *Harper's New Monthly Magazine*, February 1867.

O'Neil. Tim. *Mobs, Mayhem & Murder: Tales from the St. Louis Police Beat*. St. Louis, MO: St. Louis Post-Dispatch Books, 2008.

Owens, Luncinda. "Official Founder of Washington." May 22, 2014. www.emissourian.com.

Perrysburg (OH) *Journal*.

Reddig, William M. *Tom's Town: Kansas City and the Pendergast Legend.* Columbia: University of Missouri Press, 3d pap. ed., 1991.

Rosa, Joseph G. "George Ward Nichols and the Legend of Wild Bill Hickok." *Arizona and the West* 19, no. 2 (Summer 1997): 135–62.

Slade, Paul. "It's a Frame-Up: Frankie & Johnnie." www.planetslade.com.

Springfield News-Leader.

State of Missouri v. Glenn Chernick, 278 S.W.2d 741 (Mo. 1955).

State of Missouri v. Glenn Chernick, 280 S.W.2d 56 (Mo. 1955).

State of Missouri v. Glenn Chernick, 303 S.W.2d 595 (Mo. 1957).

Steward, Dick. *Duels and the Roots of Violence in Missouri.* Columbia: University of Missouri Press, 2000.

Stiles, T.J. *Jesse James: Last Rebel of the Civil War.* New York: Vintage pap. ed., 2003.

St. Joseph Gazette.

St. Joseph News-Press.

St. Joseph News-Press/Gazette.

St. Louis Globe-Democrat.

St. Louis Magazine.

St. Louis Post-Dispatch

St. Louis Star and Times.

Topeka (KS) *Daily Capital.*

Unger, Robert. *The Union Station Massacre: The Original Sin of J. Edgar Hoover's FBI.* Kansas City, MO: Andrews McMeel Publishing, 1997.

United States v. Lisa Montgomery, 635 F.2d 1074 (8th Cir., 2011).

Vetterli, R.E. *Report of Attack at Kansas City Union Station, June 17, 1933.* Washington, D.C.: Federal Bureau of Investigation, June 27, 1933.

Washington Historical Society. "Washington Historical Timeline." www.washmohistorical.org.

Yeatman, Ted P. *Frank and Jesse James: The Story Behind the Legend.* Nashville, TN: Cumberland House Publishing Inc., 2000.

INDEX

D

F

G

H

J

R

S

T

U

V

W

Y

ABOUT THE AUTHORS

Photograph by Lennie Bolton.

Vicki Berger Erwin has been in the publishing industry for more than thirty years in various capacities, including sales, book distribution and as the owner of a bookstore in St. Charles, Missouri. She is the author of thirty books in varied genres: picture books, middle-grade mysteries and novels, local histories and true crime. James W. Erwin practiced law in St. Louis for thirty-seven years. He is the author of five books on local history.

This is their second book together. They live in Kirkwood, Missouri.